WILL APPLE

DORSET DIVES

PUBLISHED 2014 BY Red Flannel Publishing,
Plum Tree House, East Runton, Norfolk, NR27 9PH

PRINTED BY Barnwell Print Ltd. Aylsham, Norfolk

DESIGN BY Meurig Rees [reesource.co.uk]
ORIGINAL WRECK SKETCHES BY John Liddiard*
*ILLUSTRATED BY Meurig Rees
MAPS BY Bryan Jones

FACEBOOK: Discover UK Diving
INSTAGRAM: willappleyard

CONTENTS

CONTENTS

FOREWORD

Easter 1969 at Chesil Cove was a day of sideways sleet and the day that I became a diver and truly alive. The cool water rushing into my homemade wetsuit on that first dive announced that I was free in the ocean – the world's largest, least understood, most powerful ecosystem.

I dive in some of the most remote, challenging and desirable locations and yet when I get asked about my favourite dive area I always say Dorset and it's not just for sentimental reasons: The diving is wonderfully varied and runs from easy shore dives to challenging wrecks and always includes stacks of beautiful life. You can dive in most sea conditions and it's well supported with dive shops, charter boats, boat launch areas, it's easy to get to and has some of the greatest cafés in the world. The coastline itself is the pride of Britain and adds beauty and energy to the diving experience.

I use any opportunity to dive in Dorset and you'll find me in the water, on the beach, on the dive boat or reading this book in the café!

Paul Rose

INTRODUCTION

This book should be considered a personal guide to scuba diving some of Dorset's most desirable dive sites, all of which are within easy reach for the recreational diver.

Dorset's diving is so varied - you may find yourself bagging scallops for tea on Lulworth Banks on one dive, exploring the ghostly wreck of the M2 submarine on the next, or find yourself speeding along the perilous Peveril Ledges (ranked Dorset's number one gnarliest drift dive) on another.

Scuba diving along the Dorset coastline is not just about the act of diving, imagine hugging miles of rugged Jurassic cliffs en route to your dive site, then lunching whilst anchored within the idyllic Lulworth Cove, before being dropped practically under Durdle Door to start your dive.

Let's get wet...

DIVE SITES

MAP: 01 [D] - DRIFT

MAP REF. / SITE / COORDINATES

01 Valentine Tanks. . . . . 50°39.450'N 01°53.400'W
02 Fleur de Lys . . . . 50°37.600'N 01°56.140'W
03 Betsy Anna . . . . 50°37.000'N 01°48.980'W
04 Carantan. . . . . 50°34.990'N 01°56.230'W
05 Kyarra . . . . 50°34.900'N 01°56.650'W
06 Castlereagh . . . . 50°34.840'N 01°56.170'W
07 Aeolian Sky . . . . 50°30.574'N 02°08.413'W
08 Arfon . . . . 50°29.842'N 02°10.444'W
09 Old Harry Rocks [D]. . 50°38.630'N 01°54.630'W
10 Swanage Pier. . . . .
11 Borgny. . . . . 50°35.450'N 01°41.730'W
12 Venezuela . . . . 50°35.770'N 01°43.370'W
13 Clan Macvey. . . . . 50°39.080'N 01°46.840'W
14 Peveril Ledges [D] . . . 50°36.410'N 01°56.170'W
15 Kimmeridge Bay . . . .
16 Black Hawk (BOW) . . . . 50°36.819'N 02°12.451'W

MAP: 02 [D] - DRIFT

MAP REF. / SITE / COORDINATES

17 Lulworth Cove & Stair Hole. . . . .
18 Durdle Door [D] . . . .
19 Lulworth Banks [D] . . 50°35.600'N 02°16.300'W
20 Alex Van Opstal. . . . . 50°32.439'N 02°16.133'W
21 Warbarrow Tout & Barge. . . . .
. . 50°36 860N 002°11 232'W
22 White Nothe [D]. . . . .
23 Brioney Victoria. . . . . . 50°36'58'N 002°20.51'W
24 Countess of Erne. . .50°35'.160'N 002°25.177'W
25 Landing Craft & Bombardon Unit . . . .
. . 50°34.419'N 02°24.986'W
26 Outer Breakwater [D] . . . .
27 The Dredger. . . . . . . 50°34.054'N 002°25.491'W
28 Balaclava Bay. . . . .
29 Binnendijk . . . . 50°32.122'N 02°20.088'W
30 Elena R . . . . .50°29.956 'N 002°20.658'W
31 Pulpit Rock [D] . . . . . . 50°30.630'N 02°27.800'W
32 Aerials [D] . . . .
33 James Fennell . . . . . 50°32.761'N 002°27.388'W
34 Gertrude . . . . 50°32.819'N 02°27.242'W
35 Chesil Cove. . . . .
36 Royal Adelaide. . . . . 50°34.652'N 002°28.535'W
37 UB74 . . . . 50°31.816'N 02°33.433'W
38 HMS M2 . . . . 50°34.612'N 02°33.984'W
39 Frognor . . . . 50°32.028'N 02°33.131'W

MAP: 03 [D] - DRIFT

MAP REF. / SITE / COORDINATES

40 Gibel Hamam . . . . 50°35'.851N 002° 53'.037'W
41 Saw Tooth Ledges [D]. 50°40.86'N 002°48.15'W
42 Heroine. . . . . .50°40'.532'N 002°56'.131W
43 Lanes Ground Reef [D]. . . . .
. . 50°40.46'N 002°54.94'W
44 Tenants Reef - East [D]. 50°39.12'N 02°52.75'W
45 Tenants Reef - West [D] 50°38.82'N 02°57.70'W
46 West Bay High Ground [D]. . . . .
. . 50°42.40'N, 002° 48.91'W
47 St Dunstan . . . . 50°38.296'N 02°42.050'W
48 SS Moidart . . . . 50°34.043'N 02°47.282'W
49 Baygitano . . . . 50°41.787'N 02°56.051'W
50 Golden Cap Boulder Field [D] . . . .

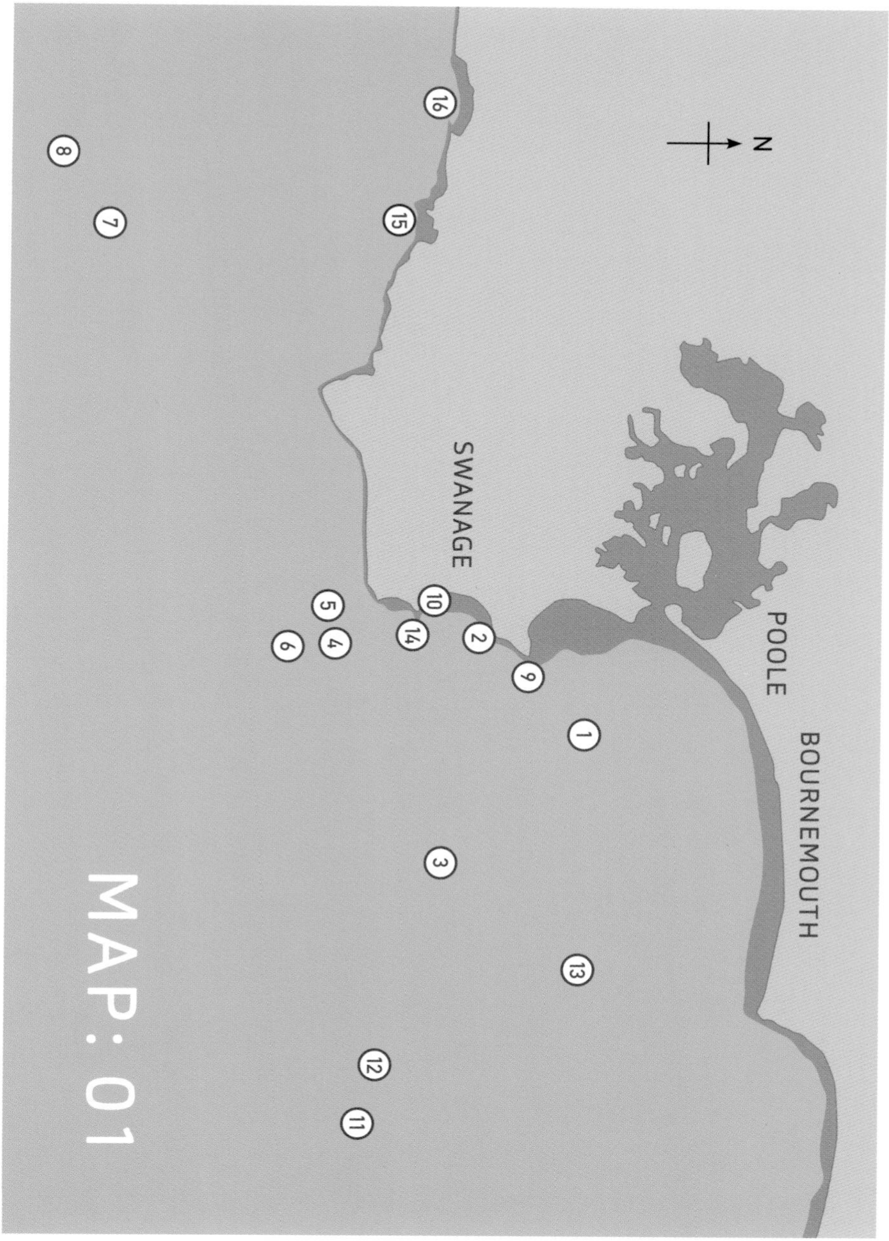
MAP: 01
N
SWANAGE
POOLE
BOURNEMOUTH
1
2
3
4
5
6
7
8
9
10
11
12
13
14
15
16

MAP: BRYAN JONES

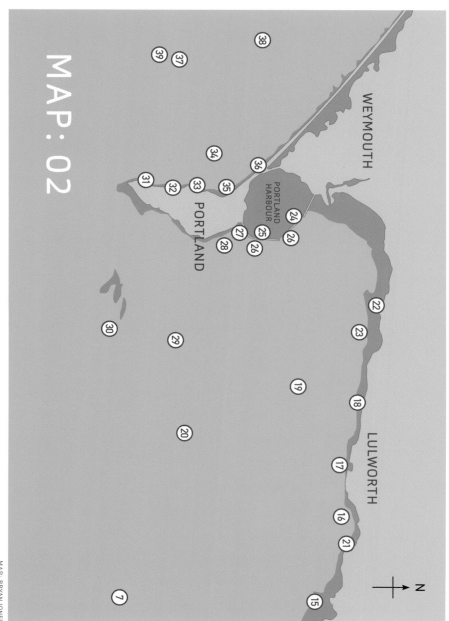

MAP: 02

WEYMOUTH

PORTLAND

PORTLAND HARBOUR

LULWORTH

N

MAP: BRYAN JONES

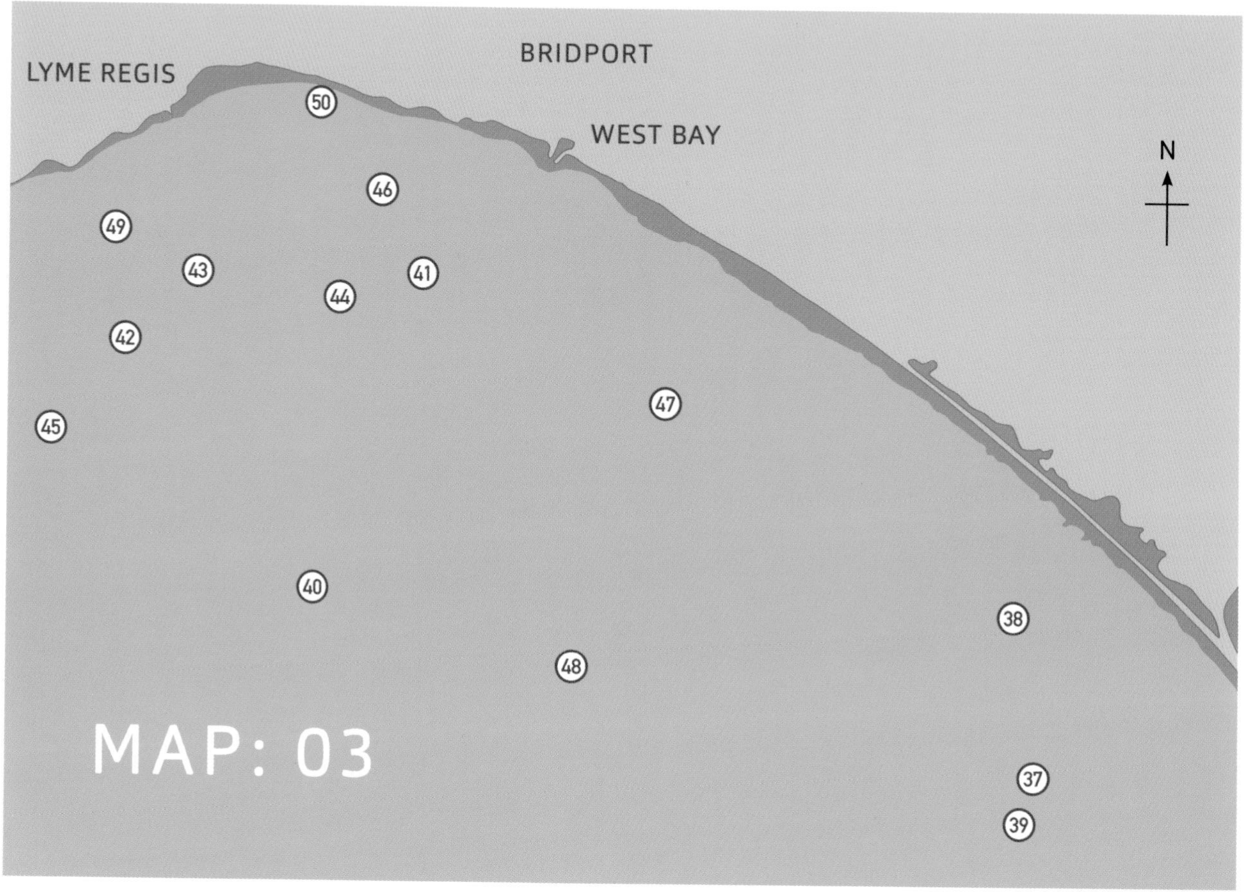

MAP: 03

LYME REGIS

BRIDPORT

WEST BAY

㊻ 45
㊾ 49
㊷ 42
㊸ 43
㊿ 50
㊵ 40
㊹ 44
㊻ 46
㊶ 41
㊽ 48
㊼ 47
㊳ 38
㊲ 37
㊴ 39

N

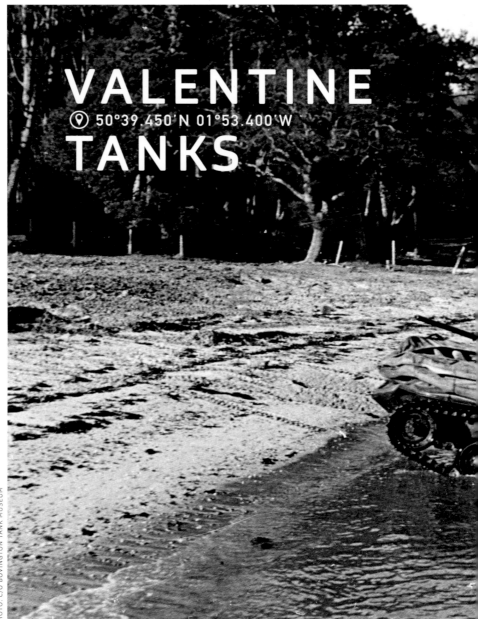

VALENTINE
◉ 50°39.450'N 01°53.400'W
TANKS

VALENTINE TANKS

50°39.450'N 01°53.400'W

Location
3.5 miles from Swanage

Getting There
Choose either Swanage or Poole based dive centres

Depth
15 metres

Things to look out for
Plaice on the sandy seabed, lone Lump Sucker, the harbour wall and of course the Tanks!

Dive blown out?
Unable to dive the Valentine Tanks? Bovington Tank Museum *tankmuseum.org*

We usually associate wrecks found on the seabed with sea going sailing vessels or motorboats, so it may appear odd that just a short boat ride from Swanage or Poole, it is possible to dive on the remains of several WWII tanks. Well, in fact these tanks were indeed seagoing vessels in their own right as they were fitted with retractable canvas frames that, when raised and the tank driven into the sea, displaced enough water to enable them to float. Known as DD Valentine Tanks (duplex drive) they were driven forward in the sea by two propellers at the rear. These particular tanks were to be used for the D Day invasions during WWII. Not surprisingly these vessels were not particularly stable in rough seas, which is why this particular pair now sit in 15 metres

PHOTO: ROB ROSLYN

PHOTO: ROB ROSLYN

of water on the seabed. The dive site is home to large schools of bib and there are one of two decent sized conger eels residing here also. Look carefully and you will be able to spot the common prawn guarding its crevice (for want of a better expression). Present the prawn with a bare hand and you may be treated to a free manicure as this diver was (pictured). Care should be taken with your buoyancy to avoid reducing the visibility for yourself and others diving the site with you.

FLEUR DE LYS

⊙ 50°37.600N, 01°56.140W

FLEUR DE LYS

50°37.600N, 01°56.140W

PHOTO: WILL APPLEYARD

Location
Swanage, between Old Harry Rocks and Swanage bay – access by boat only.

Getting There
Quickest route – Swanage based dive centres or slipway

Depth
14 metres

Things to look out for
Shoals of bib on the wreck, thorn backed rays off the wreck.

Dive blown out?
Too rough to dive Old Harry Rocks? Cycle over them instead! *britishcycling.org.uk*

The "Fleur de Lys" was a French fishing crabber, built in Brittany in 1969 that apparently sank owing to an explosion in her engine room on 16th April 2000. The permanently shot wreck is fairly broken up, although parts of the wooden hull are still recognisable – but for how long? Who knows? Sitting upright in 14 metres of water the wreck is home to an abundance of life from springtime through summer months. Shoals of bib, solitary John Dory and lobster have all colonised the Fleur de Lys. Tip: try to be the first divers in the water and on the wreck if your dive boat is busy – it does not take too many divers with wrongly placed fins to spoil the visibility here. There is often a slight current running over the wreck, which means after 15 minutes or so exploring, you can leave the wreck to enjoy a gentle drift adding variety to the dive. The wreck itself is quite small so after a couple of laps of it you will be ready to look elsewhere. Away from the wreckage the seabed is reasonably featureless although the marine life is there – so keep your eyes peeled and you may stumble across a thorn back ray or

two settled on the sand. Edible and velvet swimming crabs also frequent the area as well as the odd scallop. Look out for lemon sea slugs as well as tiny leach's spider crabs (think Monster Munch) guarding snakelock anemone and the masked crab half buried in the seabed looking up and waving its claws. Both crab species are plentiful here. Once you have completed your dive and back aboard the boat there will be just enough time to remove your hood and gloves before arriving back in Swanage as the boat ride is a short one.

BETSY

⊙ 50°37.000'N 01°48.980'W

ANNA

BETSY ANNA

50°37.000'N 01°48.980'W

Location
5 miles from Swanage

Getting There
Boats from Swanage or Poole

Depth
25 metres

Things to look out for
Bow and stern sections are impressive. The boilers and their resident conger eels.

Dive blown out?
Ringwood Brewery
Ringwoodbrewery.co.uk

PHOTO: ROB ROSLYN

Built on the Tyne in 1882, the Betsy Anna almost escaped a life as a dive site, as she was on tow to Cowes for repair after running in to rocks at Prawle Point in Devon. The damage together with a gale won however and after taking on enough water on tow, she sank five miles off the coast of Swanage on October 26th 1926. Today divers with a reasonable amount of experience can explore her in an accessible 25 metres of water. The most dramatic areas to explore will be the bow and stern sections and the area surrounding the boilers. Prominent sections of the former steam ships working parts are still visible including the cargo winch, bollards, the anchor winch and exposed ribs. The wreck lays on a gravel sea bed and the visibility is forever changing. Dive her on a good visibility day with lots of ambient light and you could spend all day on her. Pack a hefty torch however and assume that this could not be the case. The vessel was 206ft long and seldom teaming with divers who prefer their wrecks closer to shore.

Prominent sections of the former steam ships working parts are still visible

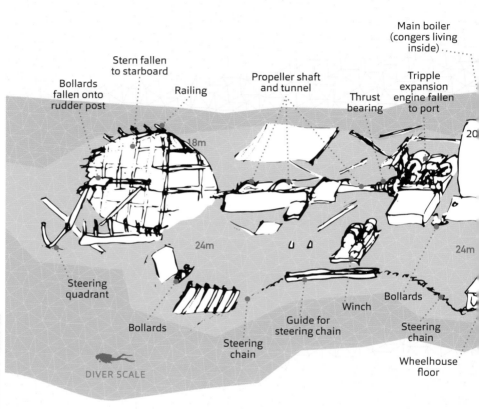

Main boiler (congers living inside)

Stern fallen to starboard

Bollards fallen onto rudder post

Railing

Propeller shaft and tunnel

Thrust bearing

Tripple expansion engine fallen to port

18m

20

24m

24m

Steering quadrant

Bollards

Winch

Bollards

Guide for steering chain

Steering chain

Steering chain

Wheelhouse floor

DIVER SCALE

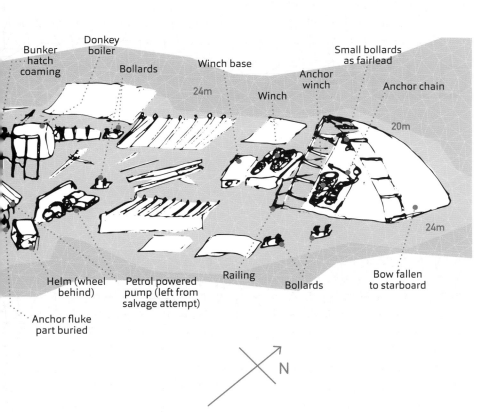

Bunker
hatch
coaming

Donkey
boiler

Bollards

24m

Winch base

Winch

Anchor
winch

Small bollards
as fairlead

Anchor chain

20m

24m

Helm (wheel
behind)

Petrol powered
pump (left from
salvage attempt)

Railing

Bollards

Bow fallen
to starboard

Anchor fluke
part buried

N

BETSY ANNA

50°37.000'N 01°48.980'W

CARANTAN

 50°34.990'N 01°56.230'W

CARANTAN

50°34.990'N 01°56.230'W

Location
Swanage

Getting There
Boat charter or launching from Swanage – only minutes away.

Depth
29 metres

Things to look out for
The prop shaft, toilet & basin.

Dive blown out?
Knock a few balls about –
Pirate Adventure Mini Golf
SAT NAV - DT4 7SX

What seems like only yards from Dorset's rock star dive site the Kyarra, what is left of the 120ft Carantan lays on her port side in 29 metres of water. Much of the remaining wreckage is hidden beneath the sand, but what is still visible is worth investigating. The Carantan worked as a French submarine chaser in WWII and capsized and sank on 21st December 1943. Theories suggest she capsized owing to her weighty top-heavy brass construction. At the time of writing a permanent shot line aids divers on to the wreck – the rope being tied into the propeller shaft that makes up much of the wreck. On reaching the dive site, follow the prop shaft and you will reach the diesel engine and to one side of the ship's toilet and the basin have spilled onto the sand. Follow the prop shaft heading away from the engine and drop off the end and you will discover some of the remaining depth charges – used to do away with German U Boats. The dive site is reasonably small and would suit no more than one boatload of divers at a time. The (usually) permanent shot line means that your return to the surface can be made effortlessly. A standard 12-litre cylinder of 21% breathing air will be plenty for this dive, owing to the reasonably smallish area the diver has available to explore.

The (usually) permanent shot line means that your return to the surface can be made effortlessly.

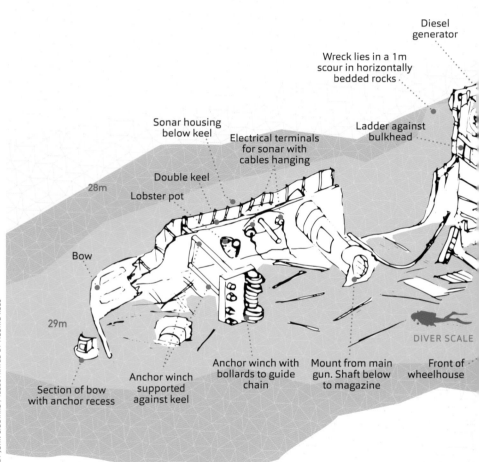

Diesel generator

Wreck lies in a 1m scour in horizontally bedded rocks

Sonar housing below keel

Electrical terminals for sonar with cables hanging

Ladder against bulkhead

Double keel

28m

Lobster pot

Bow

29m

Section of bow with anchor recess

Anchor winch supported against keel

Anchor winch with bollards to guide chain

Mount from main gun. Shaft below to magazine

Front of wheelhouse

DIVER SCALE

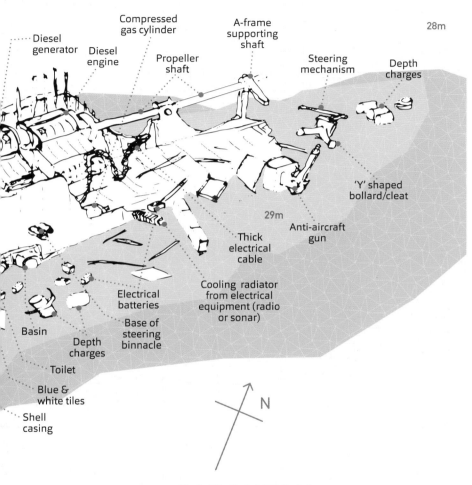

Diesel
generator

Compressed
gas cylinder

Diesel
engine

A-frame
supporting
shaft

28m

Propeller
shaft

Steering
mechanism

Depth
charges

'Y' shaped
bollard/cleat

29m

Anti-aircraft
gun

Thick
electrical
cable

Cooling radiator
from electrical
equipment (radio
or sonar)

Electrical
batteries

Basin

Depth
charges

Base of
steering
binnacle

Toilet

Blue &
white tiles

Shell
casing

N

CARANTAN

50°34.990'N 01°56.230'W

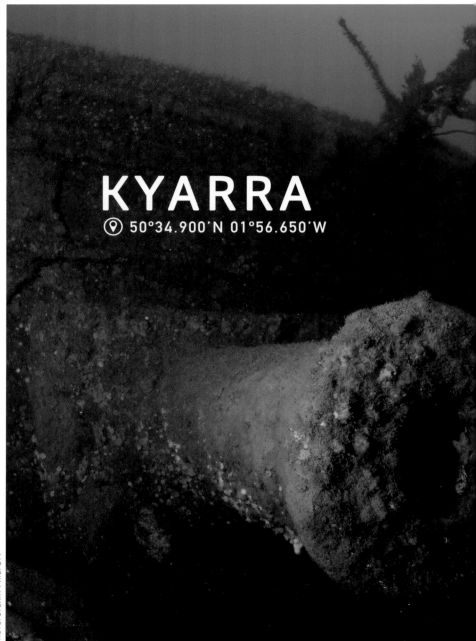

KYARRA

⊙ 50°34.900'N 01°56.650'W

KYARRA

50°34.900'N 01°56.650'W

Location
Swanage

Getting There
Only a few minutes boat ride
from Swanage, so near you
will barely have time to kit up!

Depth
23 – 32 metres

Things to look out for
check out the cabinet in Divers
Down shop for an idea

Dive blown out?
Stick your walking boots on
hengistburyhead.org

PHOTO: STUART PHILPOTT

Probably one of the most famous wrecks along the Dorset coast, local dive centres will never have trouble filling a boat when advertising a trip here. The dive site suits advanced divers and above and in good visibility is an exciting dive, so dive her after a period of good weather and you will be in for a treat. Much like the Red Sea's "Thistlegorm", on a summer's day boats flock to the wreck from all around (ok, perhaps the Thistlegorm was a mild exaggeration, but it can get busy). The Kyarra, famous for its brass fixtures and fittings aplenty, was a Scottish built steam ship produced for the Australasian United Steam Navigation Company and was packed full of all kinds of goodies along with hundreds of Australian soldiers and the odd civilian. She was en route to Sydney Australia but sent to the bottom by UB-57 on May 26th 1918 near Anvil Point, Isle of Purbeck. The wreck has thrown up some interesting finds over the years, however having been dived continuously since its discovery in the 1960's perhaps much of the really interesting stuff has already been pilfered. However, it is said that her holds do still contain perfume, wine and champagne bottles, porcelain teeth, fabrics and gold, silver & brass watches and medical supplies to name a few items. The wreck, owned by Kingston BSAC, is 126 metres long so a beast of a dive site and therefore spacious enough to accommodate several boat loads of divers at once. Often divers are dropped amidships where one

of its four boilers can be clearly seen just away from the main wreckage, the other three boilers remain inside. You will find the seabed at around 32 metres and the highest piece of metal at 23 metres making this a decent nitrox dive or a short-ish air dive. There are plenty of penetrable areas along the length of the wreck, however extra care should be taken during low visibility. The Kyarra still boast many recogisable features including winching equipment, the propeller shafts, railings, chains and bollards. Tip: The site should be dived during slack water, one hour before and six hours after Dover high water and is a very short boat ride away from Swanage based dive centres.

PHOTO: WILL APPLEYARD

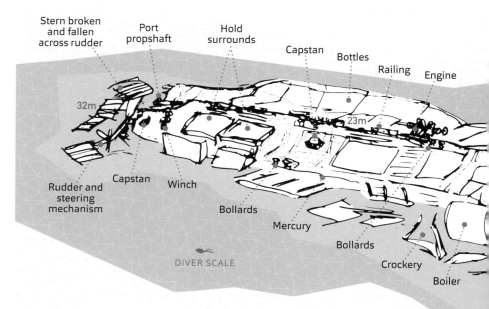

Stern broken and fallen across rudder

Port propshaft

Hold surrounds

Capstan

Bottles

Railing

Engine

32m

23m

Rudder and steering mechanism

Capstan

Winch

Bollards

Mercury

Bollards

Crockery

Boiler

DIVER SCALE

ORIGINAL SKETCH BY JOHN LIDDIARD / ILLUSTRATED BY MEURIG REES

N ↗

KYARRA

50°34.900'N 01°56.650'W

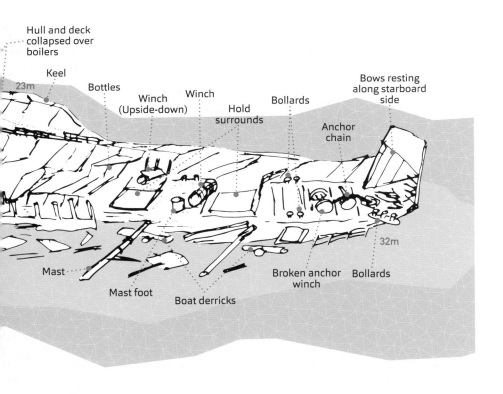

Hull and deck collapsed over boilers

Keel

23m

Bottles

Winch (Upside-down)

Winch

Hold surrounds

Bollards

Bows resting along starboard side

Anchor chain

32m

Mast

Mast foot

Boat derricks

Broken anchor winch

Bollards

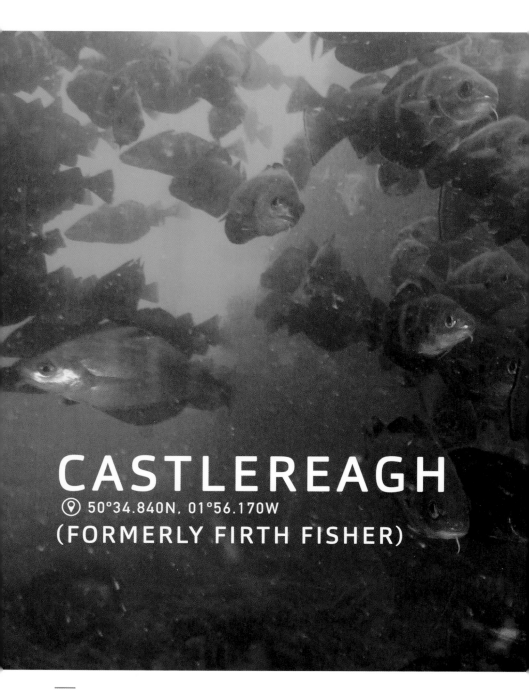

CASTLEREAGH
◉ 50°34.840N, 01°56.170W
(FORMERLY FIRTH FISHER)

CASTLEREAGH
(FORMERLY FIRTH FISHER)
50°34.840N, 01°56.170W

Location
Swanage

Getting There
Boat charter or launching from
Swanage will be your quickest route.
12 miles from Poole.

Depth
33 metres

Things to look out for
It is upright! The bow, boilers & stern.

Dive blown out?
Extreme everything – Gorcombe
Extreme Sports
Gorcombe.co.uk

Feel the urge to dive on an upright, recognisable ship shaped wreck? You can satisfy that urge here – just try and dive here on a good visibility day. This wreck is often listed on dive centre schedules by her former name "Firth Fisher" - the Castlereagh was the name given to her when sold to John Kelly & Co. by John Fisher & Sons shortly after being built in 1898. She sank in February 1925 during a gale with the loss of all 11 on board en route to Shoreham from Ayr. The coaster was carrying a cargo of coal at the time. Diver Dave Weightman discovered this wreck in 1967 and recovered the bell. Ideally you will want to dive this wreck on

This wreck is often listed on dive centre schedules by her former name

PHOTO: WILL APPLEYARD

Nitrox and even in poor visibility orientation will be quite simple. The pointy end (bow) is quite obvious and an anchor sits close to it a metre or so deeper on the seabed. There is then not a huge amount to see (except the outline of the hull both port and starboard) until you reach the boilers towards to stern. The propeller has been salvaged and the rudder is no more, however it is easy to identify where these parts once lived. There are a couple of bollards present on what remains of the deck. Lots of bib and pollack hang about over the wreck site as you would expect.

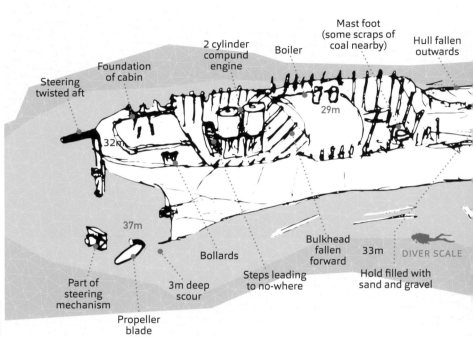

Steering
twisted aft

Foundation
of cabin

2 cylinder
compund
engine

Boiler

Mast foot
(some scraps of
coal nearby)

Hull fallen
outwards

32m

29m

37m

Part of
steering
mechanism

Propeller
blade

3m deep
scour

Bollards

Steps leading
to no-where

Bulkhead
fallen
forward

Hold filled with
sand and gravel

33m

DIVER SCALE

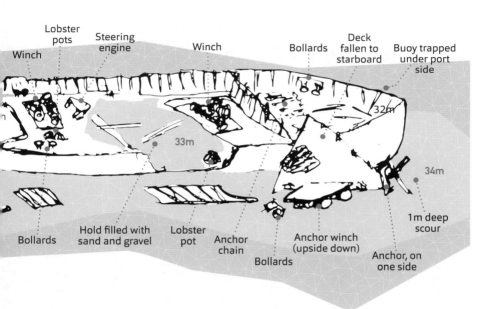

Winch · Lobster pots · Steering engine · Winch · Bollards · Deck fallen to starboard · Buoy trapped under port side

32m

33m

34m

1m deep scour

Bollards · Hold filled with sand and gravel · Lobster pot · Anchor chain · Bollards · Anchor winch (upside down) · Anchor, on one side

N

CASTLE REAGH
(FIRTH FISHER)

50°34.840N, 01°56.170W

AEOLIAN
⊙ 50°30.574'N 02°08.413'W
SKY

AEOLIAN SKY

50°30.574′N 02°08.413′W

Location
In reasonably equal distance from
Swanage, Portland or Weymouth

Getting There
Boats or launch from Portland,
Weymouth or Swanage

Depth
18 - 28 metres

Things to look out for
Land Rovers, small glass bottles
in nooks and crannies.

Dive blown out?
Check out some kite surfing
action. It is all the rage along
the east side of Chesil Beach.
paracademyextreme.co.uk

*Parts of the Sky are
penetrable including
the engine room, however,
caution should be taken...*

PHOTO: WILL APPLEYARD

This monster of a Greek freighter was carrying "general cargo" when she sank in 1979 one day after colliding with the German vessel Anna Knuppel during bad weather. The crew was helicoptered to safety. After the sinking, salvage divers recovered many items including the propeller and it is said that a million Seychelles rupee bank notes were stored in her sickbay and that many still remain missing today. Being such a huge vessel and loaded with such an array of cargo from Land Rovers, trucks, tractors, drums containing chemicals and glass bottles, the Aeolian Sky has made for an exciting wreck to dive over the years. The Aeolian Sky is what I would call a proper wreck, laying on her port side with many of the boat's features very much still recognisable including winches, railings and the funnel. Parts of the Sky are penetrable including the engine room, however, caution should be taken when attempting to do this. The wreck was cleared from the surface by explosives shortly after sinking, which has produced over-hangs and a labyrinth of twisted metal remains to explore. She stands quite proud of the seabed with the shallowest parts being between 18-20 metres and the seabed at around 28 metres.

The outer part of the hull is now covered with marine life and almost resembles a sloping seabed, however once you have reached the top or deck level, you will soon get your bearings again. Visibility can be exceptional after a spell of good weather reaching up to 15 metres. When the visibility is this good, expect a super dive and if possible dive it with nitrox in your tank to maximize your time there. Failing that, come and explore it for a second or third time with a cylinder of your favorite breathing air. Visibility is often better at high water slack.

PHOTO: ROB ROSLYN

PHOTO: ROB ROSLYN

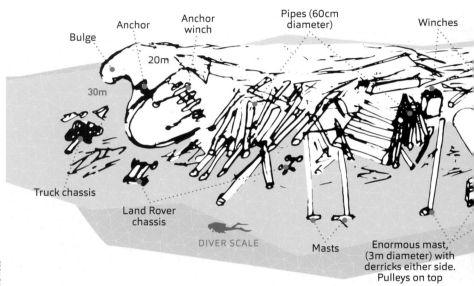

Bulge

Anchor

Anchor winch

Pipes (60cm diameter)

Winches

20m

30m

Truck chassis

Land Rover chassis

DIVER SCALE

Masts

Enormous mast, (3m diameter) with derricks either side. Pulleys on top

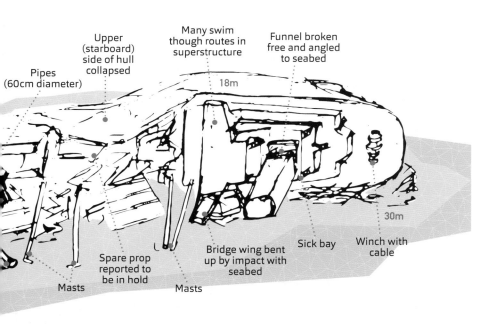

Pipes
(60cm diameter)

Upper
(starboard)
side of hull
collapsed

Many swim
though routes in
superstructure

Funnel broken
free and angled
to seabed

18m

30m

Spare prop
reported to
be in hold

Bridge wing bent
up by impact with
seabed

Sick bay

Winch with
cable

Masts

Masts

AEOLIAN SKY

50°30.574'N 02°08.413'W

ARFON

📍 50°29.842'N 02°10.444'WV

ARFON

50°29.842'N 02°10.444'W

Location
7 miles south of
Warbarrow Bay

Getting There
Boats or launch from either
Portland, Weymouth, Swange
or Poole – it is reasonably
central to all.

Depth
32 - 35 metres

Things to look out for
Propeller, boilers, your
bottom time

Dive blown out?
The Red Sea instead then?
Blueotwo.com

it is essential that you are comfortable diving to 35 metres in a potentially dark and gloomy environment

PHOTO: ROB ROSLYN

The Arfon (Welsh for "facing Angelsey")
began life as a fishing trawler and brought
into service by the Navy during WW1 to begin
life as a minesweeper. Tragically it was the
mine she did not sweep that destroyed her
and took the lives of her 10 crew on 30th
April 1917. Mine laying U boat UC61 was
the culprit and had a total of 15 successes to
its name, lead by commander Georg Gerth.
To dive the Arfon a reasonable amount of
experience is required with the shallowest
point being the boilers at 32 metres. You
will not want to spend the duration of the
dive sitting on these, so it is essential that
you are comfortable diving to 35 metres in
a potentially dark and gloomy environment.
The propeller is worth a look and the wreck
site in general is alive with shoaling fish and
wriggling with crustaceans.

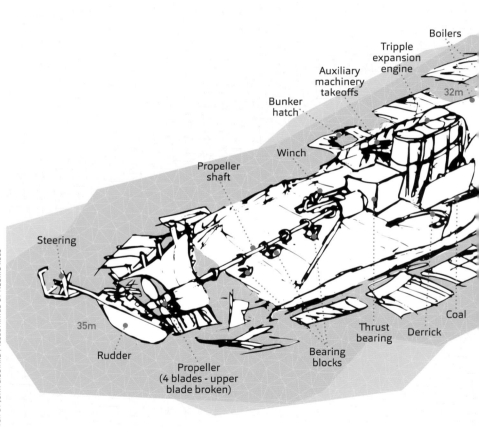

Boilers

Tripple expansion engine

Auxiliary machinery takeoffs

32m

Bunker hatch

Winch

Propeller shaft

Steering

35m

Coal

Thrust bearing

Derrick

Rudder

Propeller (4 blades - upper blade broken)

Bearing blocks

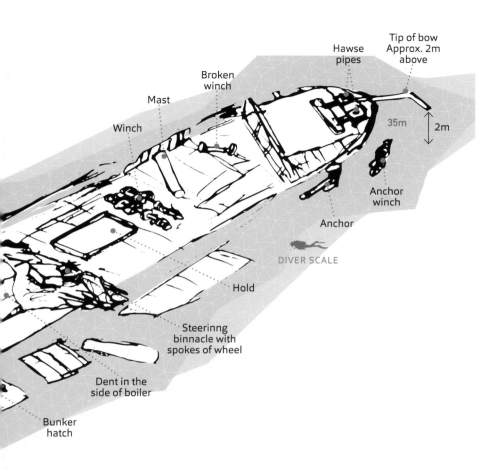

Tip of bow
Approx. 2m
above

Hawse
pipes

Broken
winch

Mast

Winch

35m

2m

Anchor
winch

Anchor

DIVER SCALE

Hold

Steerinng
binnacle with
spokes of wheel

Dent in the
side of boiler

Bunker
hatch

N

ARFON

50°29.842'N 02°10.444'W

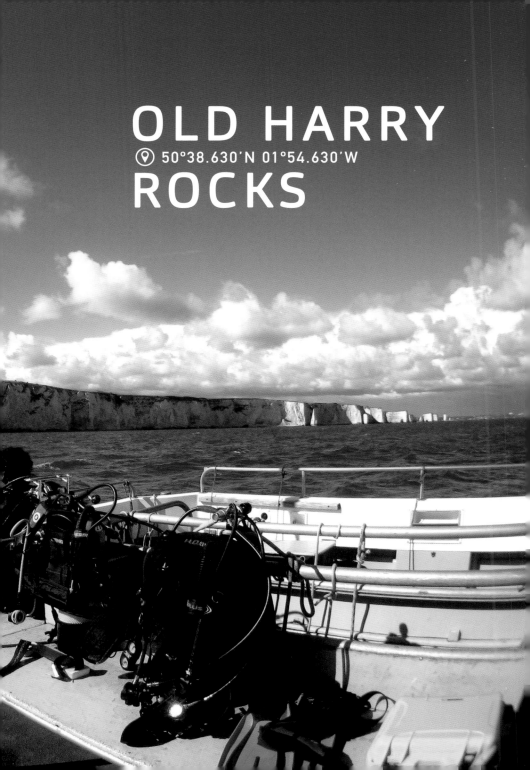

OLD HARRY

📍 50°38.630'N 01°54.630'W

ROCKS

OLD HARRY ROCKS

50°38.630'N 01°54.630'W

Location
Handfast Point (Near Swanage and Poole)

Getting There
Short boat ride from Poole or Swanage. You cannot miss these big chalky guys.

Depth
10 – 15 metres

Things to look out for
Smooth Hound, Rays

Dive blown out?
Check out Corfe Castle on your way home from Swanage
nationaltrust.org.uk/corfe-castle

keep your eyes peeled as this spot is known for its smooth hound and undulate ray siting's.

The Old Harry rocks drift is a popular dive site only 10 minutes boat ride east of Swanage or around six miles from Poole. Two stacks of chalk make up Old Harry at Handfast Point on the Isle of Purbeck. There are two stories surrounding the rocks naming – one being that they were named after the infamous Poole pirate "Harry Paye" who once stashed his contraband near by and the other being a reference to the Devil (apparently known euphemistically as Old Harry), who, legend has it, once slept on the rocks – take your pick. The drift dive itself can be fast flowing and over a flat seabed, known as Old Harry races. While the dive itself can initially appear to be rather featureless, keep your eyes peeled as this spot is famous for its smooth hound and undulate ray siting's. You will also spot dogfish here and there about the seabed too. It is also said that Spitfire pilots would use the rocks as target practice during WWII and that their spent shells can still be found here. Be sure to pack your SMB as boat skippers will be sure to want to see it on the surface throughout your dive here.

PHOTO: ROB ROSLYN

PHOTO: ROB ROSLYN

SWANAGE PIER

SWANAGE PIER
OLD & NEW

Location
Swanage town centre

Getting There
Head for Swanage town centre, where the pier is well sign posted and can't be missed

Depth
4 - 5 metres

Things to look out for
Pipefish in the grassy areas, wrasse of various kinds, the odd tompot blenny

Dive blown out?
Tech head fun –
Royal Signals Museum
Royalsignalsmuseum.com

PHOTO: ROB ROSLYN

Easy access means that novice divers can hone their skills and become accustom to UK waters in relative safety here. Conveniently, there is a well-stocked dive centre on the pier (Divers Down) providing air fills and essential kit.

Although the pier can be dived at any time, you will make more of the limited depth if dived at high tide. Resident marine life includes plenty of ballan wrasse, blennies, anemone, crabs and from time to time - bass. Be careful when you reach the far end of the pier, as this area is popular with fishermen and a fair amount of line can be found in the water – not always attached to the end of a rod. Dive boats come and go from the left hand side of the pier too, so watch out for their propellers. Move away from the pier, to the right and you may chance upon the odd pipefish. They are very well camouflaged so a keen eye will be required to spot one hiding among the grassy patches. The seabed here is sandy and the visibility often excellent as a result.

Adjacent to the Victorian pier you will notice the remains of the "old pier"; this part is directly accessible from Divers Down's pontoon, behind the shop (seek permission from the shop to use this first). It is a brighter dive, as none of its decking remains, however this site can be busy with boat traffic so caution should be taken when on or near the surface. The area is quite weedy, making an ideal home for a variety of species. Losing your bearings is surprisingly easy owing to the curved shape of the pier's remaining posts. However it is shallow, so easy to surface and regroup if you do. Both piers are good spots to sharpen your camera, buoyancy or SMB deployment skills and the visibility is usually good.

BORGNY

📍 50°35.450'N 01°41.730'W

BORGNY

50°35.450'N 01°41.730'W

Location
South of the Needles,
Isle of Wight

Getting There
Boats from Lymington, Poole,
Swanage or Isle of Wight.

Depth
26 - 32 metres

Things to look out for
Propeller, rib swim throughs,
remains of coal cargo

Dive blown out?
You can get wet here
Newforestwaterpark.co.uk

The bow and stern sections make up the highest and most interesting areas to explore with the propeller still in place

The Borgny was just one of many coal-carrying vessels sent to the seabed by patrolling German submarines in WW1. A torpedo strike destroyed the vessel on 22nd February 1918 with no loss of life. Like many others before and after, her destination was set for Rouen in northwest France - the capital of the Haute-Normandie region. Rouen became an important location logistically in WW1 as a major base for supplies bound for the front line, hospitals and the disembarkation point for troops with a ticket to the trenches. Supply ships would cross the channel, enter the mouth of the Seine and wind their way up river before off loading their cargo or personnel.

The identification of the wreck came from Hurn SAC upon their discovery of the stern lettering. The bow and stern sections make up the highest and most interesting areas to explore with the propeller still in place (pictured) and some of the hull plates creating interesting over hangs. The exposed ribs are worth exploring too, however amidships much of the wreck is quite flat. The boiler is still there of course and some evidence of the cargo of coal can be seen about the wreck and on the sea floor. The Borgny is an ideal nitrox dive owing to her depth.

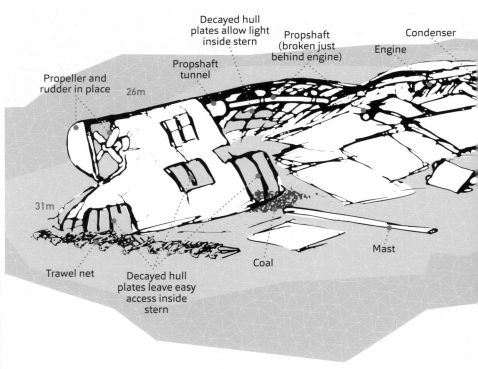

Decayed hull plates allow light inside stern

Propshaft (broken just behind engine)

Condenser

Engine

Propshaft tunnel

Propeller and rudder in place

26m

Trawel net

Decayed hull plates leave easy access inside stern

Coal

Mast

31m

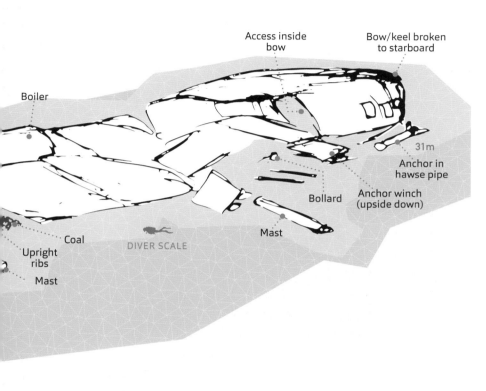

Access inside bow

Bow/keel broken to starboard

Boiler

31m

Anchor in hawse pipe

Bollard

Anchor winch (upside down)

Coal

DIVER SCALE

Mast

Upright ribs

Mast

N

BORGNY

50°35.450'N 01°41.730'W

PHOTO: WILL APPLEYARD

VENEZUELA

⊙ 50°35.770N 01°43.370W

VENEZUELA

50°35.770N 01°43.370W

Location
10 miles from Swanage

Getting There
Boats from Swanage or Poole

Depth
28 metres

Things to look out for
Boilers and triple expansion engine

Dive blown out?
Learn about some of the other U Boat victories here - *Uboat.net*

PHOTO: ROB ROSLYN

See the Borgny dive site section for information on Rouen's importance during WW1.

One of seven ships sunk by WW1 German U boat UB59, the Venezuela was en route to Rouen, France from Swansea via Falmouth carrying coal. This steam ship was sunk by torpedo on 14th March 1918 with all hands lost. See the Borgny dive site section for information on Rouen's importance during WW1. UB59 took part in five patrols in her wartime career and was later scuttled in Zebrugge during the German evacuation from Belgium.

Well broken up in 27 metres of water the main features of the wreck are the boilers and triple expansion engine. Much of the sides of the hull are still visible giving divers an idea of its ship shape. The site is quite a trek by hard boat and a journey you would only really want to make on the flattest of calm days.

PHOTO: ROB ROSLYN

PHOTO: WILL APPLEYARD

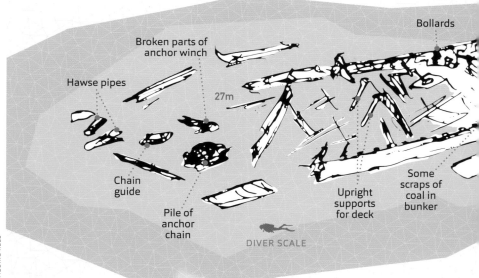

Bollards

Broken parts of
anchor winch

Hawse pipes

27m

Chain
guide

Pile of
anchor
chain

Upright
supports
for deck

Some
scraps of
coal in
bunker

DIVER SCALE

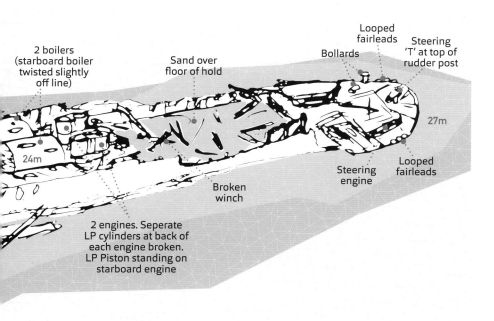

2 boilers
(starboard boiler
twisted slightly
off line)

Sand over
floor of hold

Looped
fairleads

Bollards

Steering
'T' at top of
rudder post

27m

24m

Broken
winch

Steering
engine

Looped
fairleads

2 engines. Seperate
LP cylinders at back of
each engine broken.
LP Piston standing on
starboard engine

N

VENEZUELA

50°35.770N 01°43.370W

CLAN
📍 50°39.080'N 01°46.840'W
MACVEY

CLAN MACVEY

50°39.080'N 01°46.840'W

Location
Eastern end of Poole Bay –
3 miles off shore

Getting There
Boats from Swanage or Poole

Depth
18 metres

Things to look out for
Gun, congers, plaice, sand

Dive blown out?
Check out the list of vessels
sunk by UB57
*uboat.net/wwi/boats/
successes/ub57.html*

Sand, sand and more sand! The Clan Macvey has over time has been covered with the stuff and each time you dive it, it will probably have changed slightly as a result. Often referred to as the "Clan Macsand" or simply the "Clan" by those in the know, this armed merchant ship was put here by German submarine UB57 with seven lives lost. UB57 had an impressive list of hits to her name including everybody's favourite wreck – the Kyarra. 8th August 1918 was the date she became a dive site and is now home to many conger eels and surrounded by plaice that just love this sandy environment. It is said that the ship's gun is still present and some of the wreckage stands two to four metres proud of the seabed. A reasonably shallow dive in only 18 metres of water, this is of course the perfect introductory dive for the inexperienced.

PHOTO: ROB ROSLYN

Often referred to as the "Clan Macsand" or simply the "Clan" by those in the know

PEVERIL
◉ 50°36.410'N 01°56.170'W
LEDGES

PEVERIL LEDGES

50°36.410'N 01°56.170'W

📍 Location
A few minutes boat ride from Swanage pier, just outside of the bay.

👉 Getting There
The most popular mode of transport is a boat from Swanage – just 10 minutes boat ride away.

Depth
13 – 25 metres

🥽 Things to look out for
The undulating seabed as you hold on to your SMB reel for dear life!

✋ Dive blown out?
Eat and drink in The Kings Arms pub (go in the evening and meet the locals) Langton Matravers, near Swanage.

As well as looking down, look forward to save the embarrassment of crashing into rocks at speed.

PHOTO: WILL APPLEYARD

If it is a flying experience you are after, this is the site for you. Dropping down through the water column the seabed suddenly appears at 13 metres, whizzing by beneath you at a cracking pace. Depending on where you are dropped in, divers initially descend on to a flat, reasonably featureless seabed and once the drift dive takes shape, the ledges suddenly present themselves. They are almost ramp-like in their appearance with often two or more metres of depth can be lost as you "take off". A quick glance back once over the top reveals a bank of sand and fine shingle with crabs and fish sheltering from the current. As well as looking down, look forward to save the embarrassment of crashing into rocks at speed. Before reaching the next one the drift can slow down somewhat as the current decides on which direction it is heading.

PHOTO: WILL APPLEYARD

Agree on a maximum depth before making the dive, as it can drop to 25 metres in the gullies between the ledges. If you decide to stop at 20 metres or shallower, you will find the seabed can disappear from sight at times, don't fret; it will be back in view just moments later. Owing to the yoyo effect the seabed creates, you will find yourself adjusting your buoyancy more often than one might usually - it is part and parcel of this dive site so go with it.

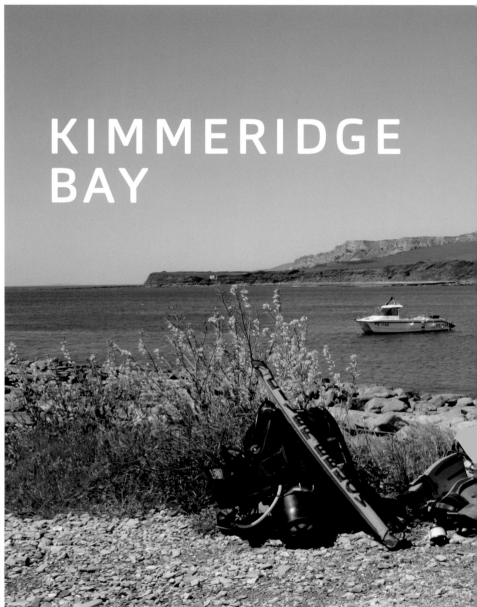

KIMMERIDGE BAY

PHOTO: WILL APPLEYARD

KIMMERIDGE BAY

Location
Kimmeridge Bay

Getting There
A351 from Wareham to Corfe Castle & the first turn right to Creech. Follow road to the top of a steep hill & round a hairbend signposted to Church Knowle. Approximately 2 miles later turn right to Kimmeridge. Drive through village to toll booth. Parking fee payable to Smedmore Estate

Depth
2 – 4 metres depending on state of tide and your location in the bay

Things to look out for
As well as your dive, take a walk round the bay looking for fossils and check out the marine centre too.

Dive blown out?
Why not go fossil hunting?
kimmeridge.ukfossils.co.uk

The rocks around Kimmeridge Bay were once part of a deep tropical sea that formed in the Jurassic period 155 million years ago. The clay cliffs surrounding the bay attract fossil hunters in their droves. A band of limestone creates a series of ledges that run out to sea. The bay itself makes for a very shallow shore dive, so best to dive on a high tide to give you more depth. Being a shallow dive there is often a slight swell, pushing you back and forth as you meander your way through rainbow wrack and coralline seaweeds. Access to the dive site is usually made via the slipway adjacent to the marine centre - a small hut by the car park, which is well worth a visit. Ballan wrasse mullet, tompot blennies and lobster can be spotted here against the almost volcanic looking sandy seabed. Tip: The visibility can be good so it is also worth snorkelling here. Kimmeridge Bay is a great all round family spot with something for everyone so worth spending the whole day here during the summer.

PHOTO: WILL APPLEYARD

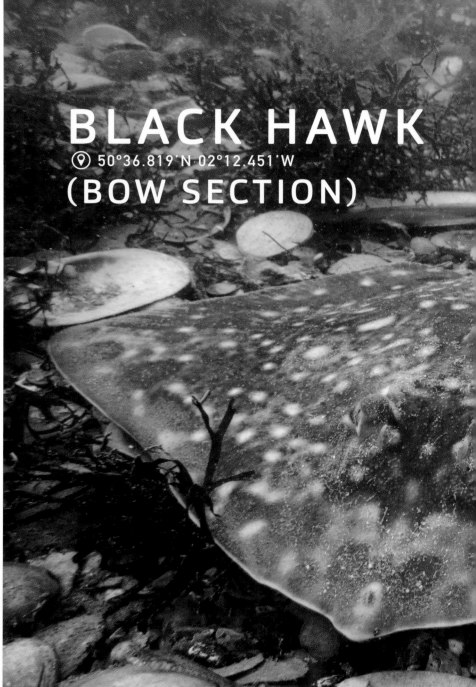

BLACK HAWK
⊙ 50°36.819'N 02°12.451'W
(BOW SECTION)

BLACK HAWK
(BOW SECTION)

50°36.819'N 02°12.451'W

Location
Warbarrow Bay

Getting There
Boats run from Portland,
Swanage & Weymouth

Depth
15 metres

Things to look out for
Check out the Winfrith pipeline
when you have finished with
the wreck.

Dive blown out?
Sometimes only the pub will
do - "the worlds most
photographed pub"
greyhoundcorfe.co.uk

The bow section of the Black Hawk sits in around 15 metres of water in Warbarrow Bay, just east of the mighty Durdle Door. This section of the vessel stayed afloat despite the rest of it being sent to the seabed by a German torpedo in 1944, closer to Portland in 40 plus metres of water. The Black Hawk was a US Liberty ship - one of many wartime cargo vessels built quickly and cheaply during World War II. She may have been more recognisable as a ship wreck today had she not been blown apart once again to clear a path for the Winfrith pipeline, located just east of the wreckage. The pipeline was laid in 1959 to take effluent from the newly constructed atomic energy site on Winfrith Heath. The pipline begins six miles inland and ends two miles out to sea. Head east when you have finished exploring the Black Hawk's remains and you will be sure to find the pipeline, measuring around 300mm in diameter. Although the wreck sits on a sandy seabed at 15 metres or so, it is possible to gain 20 metres of depth not far from the site where you may find the odd scallop and perhaps a thorn backed ray minding its own business. The Black Hawk is well broken up with parts jutting from the sand here and there. The wreck makes for an easy dive and in good weather the boat ride will be well worth the effort too, thanks due to mile upon mile of stunning scenery en route.

PHOTO: ROB ROSLYN

LULWORTH COVE & STAIR HOLE

LULWORTH COVE & STAIR HOLE

Location
Lulworth Cove

Getting There
Sat Nav BH20 5RQ / take the A352 turning onto the B3071 at Wool. Arrive before 10am if you wish to drive your gear all the way to the beach. Lots of pay and display parking just a short walk from the cove.

Depth
Shore to 9 metres

Things to look out for
Boat traffic within the cove – tow a marker buoy

Dive blown out?
Take a stroll around Lulworth Cove & lunch at *lulworth-coveinn.co.uk*

Lulworth Cove, just east of the iconic Durdle Door comprises a crescent of white pebble beach, lined with chalky white cliffs and topped with wildlife rich down-land. The cove's history dates back some 150 million years, from still visible movement in the earths crust to a Bronze Age mount sitting just outside the cove. The Celts, Romans and Anglo Saxons all occupied land here too and smugglers and pirates have also used the cove in one-way or another. Today the cove is popular with fishermen, tourist's fossil hunters, geologists, kayakers, swimmers, snorkelers and divers. As a snorkeler or diver, there are two ways to tackle the diving here – the scenic way or the gnarly way. The gnarly way consists of a hike and scramble with your gear over the southwest footpath

to your entry point at Stair Hole. Here you will find a limestone arch set in front of an idyllic little cove. From here, enter the water submerge and make your way east towards the mouth of Lulworth Cove. The seabed is made up of rocky and weedy gullies sat on sand, supporting all manner of fish life and crustaceans. The maximum depth here is around the nine-metre mark and the dive can be a long one. Only attempt this on a flat calm day and only if you have the minerals to deal with the hike to the entry point. If you are in the mood for a more leisurely diving experience, simply entering the water within Lulworth Cove and heading out into the middle is going to be more your bag. There is a lot of weed and rock to be found on the outskirts of the cove, with a sandy patch right in the middle where plaice can sometimes be spotted. Consider making your life easier still and simply pack a snorkel, mask and wet suit. Whether snorkeling or scuba diving whilst inside the cove, be sure to tow a surface marker buoy with you at all times. However you choose to spend your time at Lulworth Cove the area makes for an excellent day by the sea with miles of Jurassic coastline to scramble over either side.

there are two ways to tackle the diving here - the scenic way or the gnarly way

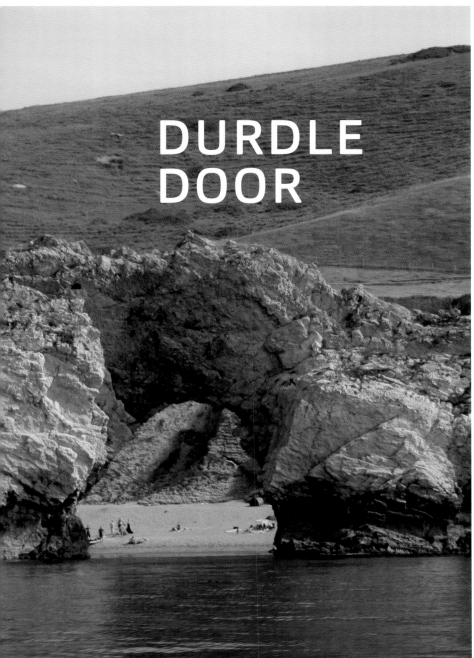

DURDLE DOOR

PHOTO: WILL APPLEYARD

DURDLE DOOR

Location
Durdle Door

Getting There
Not practical to shore dive here owing to the hike. Recommend a boat from Swanage, Portland or Weymouth.

Depth
10 - 15 metres

Things to look out for
A huge arch of limestone rock jutting out from the Dorset Coast line. Admire the beautiful shingle beaches and towering cliffs.

Dive blown out?
Check out this most famous rocky arch on foot instead –
jurassiccoast.org

PHOTO: WILL APPLEYARD

Local divers say that there is a small cave found at the end of the arch (the dragon's head end).

Surely one of the main reasons to dive at Durdle Door has to be to view this colossal natural limestone arch at close quarters from the sea. It is said that the name "Durdle" is derived from the Old English 'thirl' meaning bore or drill. Durdle Door is one of the Jurassic Coast's most iconic landmarks and the Lulworth Estate privately owns the land. Dive boats are able to put divers in the water right by the door's "entrance", by either backing up to it from a hard boat or by getting close by RIB. It is possible to start your dive close to the arch

PHOTO: ROB ROSLYN

and work your way down over a series of initially kelp covered rocky ledges that form the start of the reef, only a couple of metres from the surface. Local divers say that there is a small cave found at the end of the arch (the dragon's head end). Typically upon reaching a depth of 10 – 15 metres, divers can work their way parallel to the shoreline on a mostly sandy seabed, intermittent rocky patches and with a surface marker buoy present for the duration of the dive. The usual selection of crabs, lobsters and species of wrasee are all of course residents with cuttlefish present here at times too. Cuttlefish are often spotted here ambushing prey from rock free patches. Lulworth Cove is only round the corner too, making for a pleasant spot for anchorage at lunchtime.

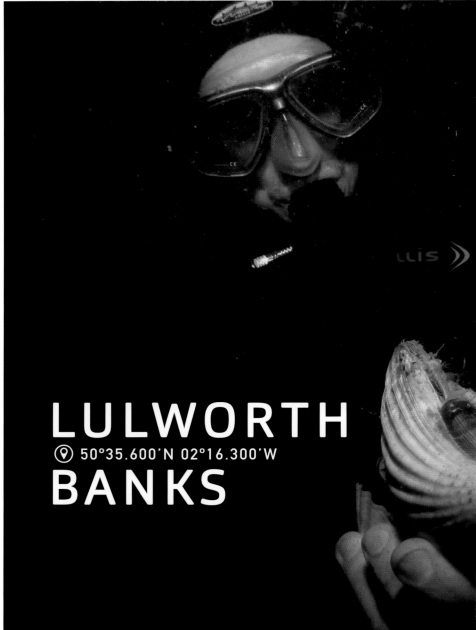

LULWORTH
⊙ 50°35.600'N 02°16.300'W
BANKS

PHOTO: ROB ROSLYN

LULWORTH BANKS

50°35.600'N 02°16.300'W

Location
Between Portland and Swanage, access by boat only

Getting There
Portland, Swanage, Weymouth based dive centres will take you.

Depth
10 - 25 metres

Things to look out for
Scallops galore, rays

Dive blown out?
Award winning outdoor adventure – Go Ape/Moors Valley
Goape.co.uk/moors-valley

PHOTO: WILL APPLEYARD

The stunning scenery en route to the site is one of the reasons to actually go and experience this dive. You feel like you are getting your money's worth if you actually enjoy the boat ride as well as the dive. The impressive Dorset cliffs and Durdle Door on a sunny day, make the boat trip out to the banks a more than pleasurable experience. The site or "banks" themselves vary in depth depending on where you are dropped and can range from around 10 – 22 or so metres in depth. The seabed can vary visually too, from sandy barren patches with not a huge amount going on, to a rocky reef system with drop offs and rugged underwater scenery. These rugged areas are often teeming with life and some divers go specifically to collect scallops, which are plentiful. Diving here in around 20 metres of water you will not only see oodles of edible sized scallops, but also the miniature tiger scallop, which, as soon as they sense a diver approaching, leap from the sea bed and appear to make a bid for the surface.

You feel like you are getting your money's worth if you actually enjoy the boat ride as well as the dive.

ALEX VAN
📍 50°32.439'N 02°16.133'W
OPSTEL

PHOTO: WILL APPLEYARD

ALEX VAN OPSTEL

50°32.439'N 02°16.133'W

Location
Almost directly opposite Lulwoth Cove and five miles off shore

Getting There
Boat charter or launching from Portland, Weymouth or Swanage

Depth
27 - 30 metres

Things to look out for
Fearless lobster, the masts and bow section

Dive blown out?
Jump on your mountain bike or go for a stroll here *moors-valley.co.uk*

PHOTO: WILL APPLEYARD

Alongside the Elena R and the Binnendijk, this Belgian cargo and passenger liner was struck by a mine laid by German U boat "U 26" at the very beginning of world war two. At the time of her destruction on September 15th 1939 Belgium remained neutral and Britain had only declared war on Germany just days before. However, mines will be mines and upon connecting with the Alex, sent her seabed-wards where she now rests just shy of 30 metres. The wreck sits on her port side and on heaps of sand, which continually shifts covering and uncovering the twisted remains. The bow section lays in quite good condition, however an area of reasonably baron sand connects this with the balance of the vessel. The baron patch in between indicates where the mine did most of its damage. The visiting diver can expect to see the vessel's many masts at several points along the wreck with plates, ribs and lots of tangled metal covering a big area. Conger eels and lots of inquisitive lobsters will be present along the way. The Alex can only be dived on slack water and if possible on a neap tide, where the visibility can often be better. Be sure to take a torch and SMB's will be essential for your journey back to the surface.

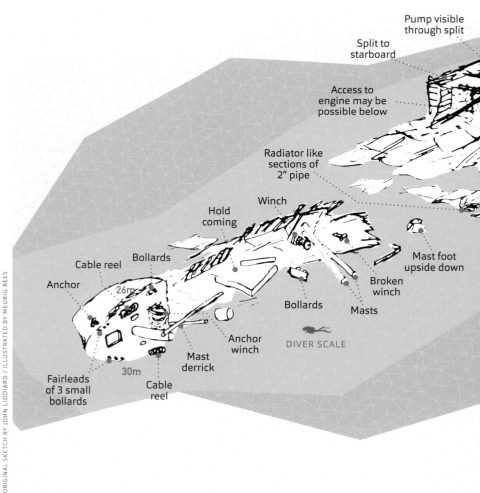

Pump visible through split

Split to starboard

Access to engine may be possible below

Radiator like sections of 2" pipe

Winch

Hold coming

Mast foot upside down

Bollards

Cable reel

Broken winch

Anchor

26m

Bollards

Masts

Anchor winch

DIVER SCALE

Mast derrick

Fairleads of 3 small bollards

30m

Cable reel

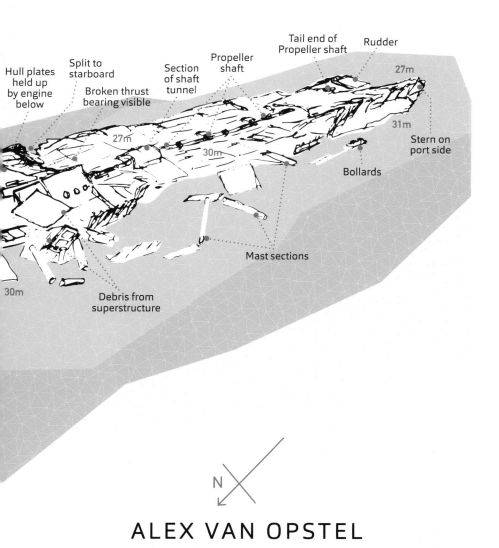

Hull plates
held up
by engine
below

Split to
starboard

Broken thrust
bearing visible

Section
of shaft
tunnel

Propeller
shaft

Tail end of
Propeller shaft

Rudder

27m

31m

Stern on
port side

Bollards

27m

30m

30m

Mast sections

Debris from
superstructure

30m

N

ALEX VAN OPSTEL

50°32.439'N 02°16.133'W

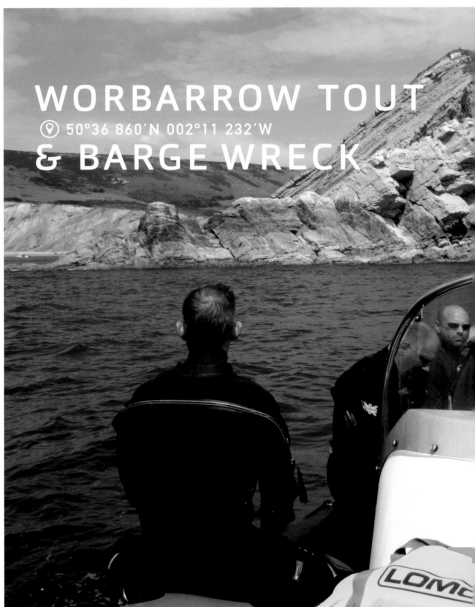

WORBARROW TOUT
50°36 860'N 002°11 232'W
& BARGE WRECK

PHOTO: WILL APPLEYARD

WORBARROW TOUT & BARGE WRECK

50°36 860'N 002°11 232'W

Location
Worbarrow Tout – Southern side

Getting There
Seven miles by boat from Portland harbour – just over the same again from Swanage. Take a RIB on a flat calm day for speed.

Depth
6 – 12 metres

Things to look out for
The barge, super sized boulders, spent tank ordinance.

Dive blown out?
Durlston Country Park. It stretches along the coast on the Isle of Purbeck at Durlston

During the height of summer this dive will not disappoint.

A true gem of a dive site and totally underrated. This site combines a great lump of obvious and recognisable wreckage along side a vibrant rocky habitat. During the height of summer this dive will not disappoint. Start your dive over the wreck of a former barge of which one side, its bow and stern and part of the deck and hatch are still largely intact. The metal stands a good three metres proud of the sea floor. The wreck lays parallel to Worbarrow Tout, which makes up the seaward end of Worbarrow Bay and is situated only yards from the shore. The remains of the inside of the barge are worth a look, with big conger spotted and fish life taking shelter among the remains. Sitting in only 12 metres of water provides the diver with ample natural light and an ideal environment for the beginner. Venture off

the wreck and towards the Tout (head north) and the scenery changes again. Giant rocks and boulders make up the next part of the dive, with many of them creating interesting caves to peer into. Head east or west to follow the labyrinth of rock and you will be sure to find spent tank ordinance laying on the seabed from the firing ranges. There is easily enough to keep the diver occupied for an hour here and a safety stop can be enjoyed on the rocks in shallower water when it is time to leave. As with much of the inshore diving along the Dorset coast, half of the enjoyment of this dive is time spent above the waves absorbing the spectacular scenery.

WHITE NOTHE

PHOTO: WILL APPLEYARD

WHITE NOTHE

Location
Ringstead Bay, east of
Weymouth

Getting There
By boat from either Weymouth
or Portland. Head east and
head towards the obelisks
sitting high on the cliff.

Depth
Shore to 10 metres

Things to look out for
Turbot, scallops, critters among
rock formations

Dive blown out?
Check out White Nothe from
the coastal path

White Nothe (meaning white nose) juts out from a beautiful chalk headland at the eastern end of Ringstead Bay. From the sea the site is easily identifiable by the pair of obelisks sat high on the grassy cliff top. These obelisks were once used as naval navigational marks. The dramatic towering white cliffs provide a splendid backdrop to what promises to be a pleasant dive for all. Diving in ten metres of water here will be all you need and if dived with a current running makes for an easy and interesting drift. The sandy seabed provides the perfect habitat for Turbot and plaice with scallops present at this depth also. A patchwork of rock and sandy gullies make up the sea floor with the rocks becoming fewer as your venture deeper. The deep you go, the more scallops appear here.

PHOTO: WILL APPLEYARD

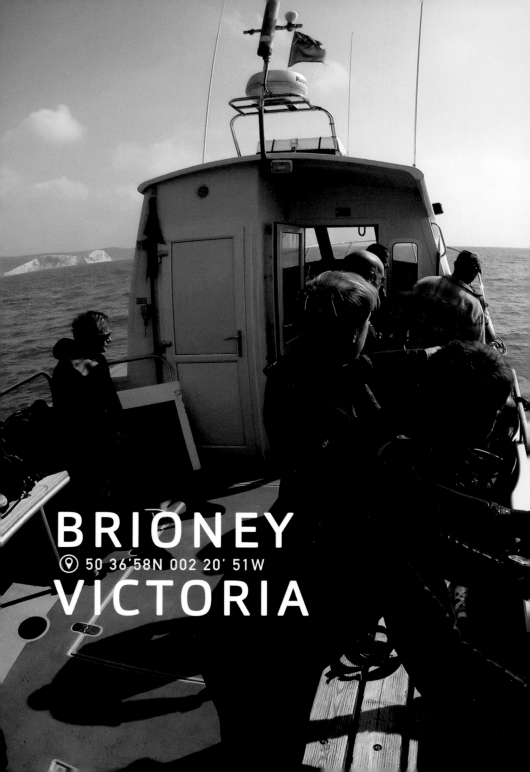

BRIONEY
⊙ 50 36'58N 002 20' 51W
VICTORIA

BRIONEY VICTORIA
"REEF" - ART INSTALLATION
50 36'58N 002 20' 51W

PHOTO: WILL APPLEYARD

Location
Ringstead Bay

Getting There
A mile and a half off Ringstead beach. Three miles from Weymouth.

Depth
21 metres (17 metres to the wheel house)

Things to look out for
Art!

Dive blown out?
Watch the footage from the comfort of your own home.
reeflive.org/the-reef-project

This is a former fishing boat now resting on the seabed, however a "wreck" it is not! This is in fact an art installation by Simon Faithfull - a contemporary artist whose work has been exhibited extensively around the world. co-commissioned by Fabrica and Photoworks, in partnership with Musée des Beaux Arts, Calais and the FRAC Basse Normandie (Caen). The "REEF" project is collaboration between artists, art organisations, marine industries and divers. The installation, a concrete clad form of a 45-foot fishing vessel sits upright on the seabed in 21 metres of water with the wheelhouse at 17 metres. Five video cameras were installed on the project when sunk in 2014. The video cameras send a real time transmission of underwater footage, which can be viewed from the comfort of your armchair at www.reeflive.org (at the time of writing). The purpose of the live feed is to demonstrate the installation's transformation from a boat into an artificial reef. A yellow buoy housing the solar panels for the cameras marks the wreck site. Divers are asked to give the cameras a wide birth so that non-divers viewing the footage can enjoy this evolving habitat too.

COUNTESS
 50 35.160 N 002 25.177 W
OF ERNE

COUNTESS OF ERNE

50 35.160 N 002 25.177 W

Location
Just inside Portland Harbour - east

Getting There
Being inside the harbour wall, Portland or based dive centres are closest. Launch your own boat from Portland.

Depth
10 – 15 metres

Things to look out for
Lump suckers in early spring, the huge rudder, squat lobster hiding in nooks and crannies and the swim through.

Dive blown out?
Still looking for action?
dorsetsnowsportcentre.co.uk

The Countess of Erne, 80 metres in length was originally a paddle steamer and in later life a coal hulk. She sank in 1935 after her moorings broke loose. The wreck today sits recognisably upright in 15 metres of water and is located only a few yards from the harbour wall between the southern and eastern entrances. A permanent mooring is usually attached to at least one end of the Countess. The wreck's deck section sits at around eight metres from the surface, making for a popular local dive. Its accessibility means that the site can become busy in peak season, although its size means

that groups can spread out, so you should only bump into one or two fellow wreckies on your way. Once you have descended onto the wreck, a lap of her hull is recommended, where you will inevitably meet her giant rudder - an excellent wide-angle photo opportunity if visibility is on your side. The Countess is penetrable in parts, however owing to the silty nature of the seabed, the visibility can quickly disappear. Tip: We would only recommend a tour inside with an experienced companion, in good visibility and of course competent buoyancy. This site is a favourite with wreck training courses. Once you have completed the lap, it is time to explore the deck area, where you will find plenty of cuckoo & ballan wrasse, rock cooks and sponges. Squat lobster and lump suckers can be found here too. Areas of the decking open up to form the holds and it is possible to drop down into these quite easily. Air permitting you should have plenty of time left for a bimble around this area, finishing the dive on the mooring line where the dive boat should pick you up. New to UK wreck diving? Then this dive site is a great place to begin.

PHOTO: WILL APPLEYARD

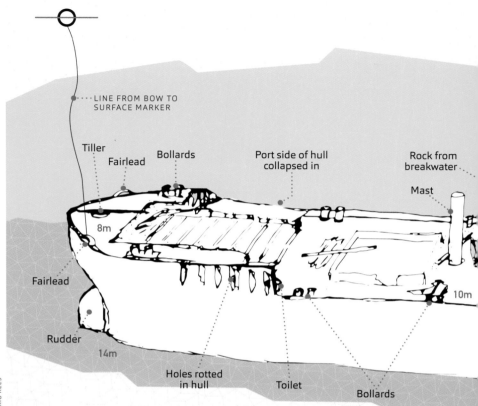

LINE FROM BOW TO
SURFACE MARKER

Tiller

Fairlead

Bollards

Port side of hull
collapsed in

Rock from
breakwater

Mast

8m

Fairlead

Rudder

14m

10m

Holes rotted
in hull

Toilet

Bollards

N

COUNTESS OF ERNE

50 35.160 N 002 25.177 W

ORIGINAL SKETCH BY JOHN LIDDIARD / ILLUSTRATED BY MEURIG REES

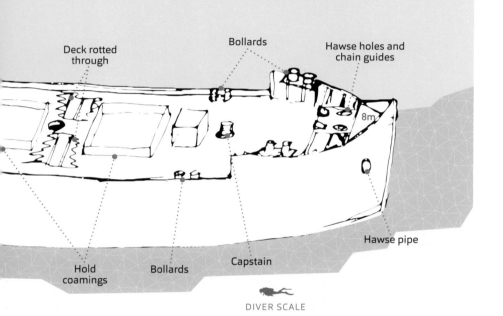

BREAKWATER

Deck rotted through

Bollards

Hawse holes and chain guides

8m

Hold coamings

Bollards

Capstain

Hawse pipe

DIVER SCALE

LANDING CRAFT &
⊙ 50.34.419N 02.24.986W
BOMBARDON UNIT

SHIRAZ

THE LANDING CRAFT & BOMBARDON UNIT

50.34.419N 02.24.986W

Location
Just inside Portland Harbour - east

Getting There
Portland based dive centres or launch for quick access.

Depth
7 – 15 metres

Things to look out for
Squid eggs, the engine, a rope guiding you between wrecks.

Dive blown out?
Burn over to Beaulieu Motor Museum
Beaulieu.co.uk

Both can be explored in one dive.

These two sites are situated in close proximity to one another, hence listing them together. They are situated at the same end of Portland harbour as the Countess of Erne and both can be explored in one dive. A rope links one to the other conveniently. The permanent shot line can be found at the bow of this WW2 landing craft, and because of the wreck's simplicity, will not take you long to explore. It is around ten metres in length, fairly intact and quite an interesting wreck, however the marine life surrounding it can be sparse. It is worth poking around nearer the seabed and around the diesel engines at the stern with your torch, but nothing much appears to live within the intact deck area itself. A rope connecting this site to the Bombardon unit can be found at the stern behind the wheelhouse and after following this for a few minutes (depending on how hard you fin) brings you to part two of the dive.

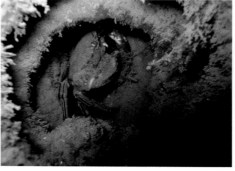

PHOTO: WILL APPLEYARD

PHOTO: WILL APPLEYARD

PHOTO: ROB ROSLYN

The Bombardon Unit, invented as a temporary pontoon and wave breaking system in WW2, makes for a reasonably interesting dive. It is around 50 metres in length with the top section at seven metres from the surface, depending on the tide. Its interesting structure allows you to peer inside with the torch and parts of it are penetrable, although I personally would not want to enter it. There are plenty of fish about, as well as the odd crab here and there. A length along the east side of the wreck and back over the top will be as much as you will want to do, before making your way back to the shot on the Landing Craft. If you do surface away from the line, swim away from the harbour wall, as the boat will not want to manoeuvre too close to it when picking divers up.

PHOTO: DAMIAN BROWN

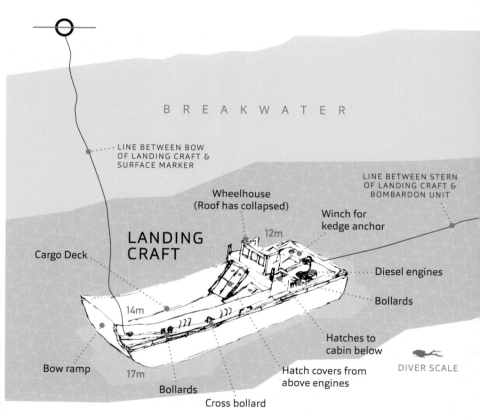

BREAKWATER

LINE BETWEEN BOW
OF LANDING CRAFT &
SURFACE MARKER

LINE BETWEEN STERN
OF LANDING CRAFT &
BOMBARDON UNIT

Wheelhouse
(Roof has collapsed)

Winch for
kedge anchor

12m

LANDING
CRAFT

Cargo Deck

Diesel engines

Bollards

14m

Hatches to
cabin below

Bow ramp

17m

DIVER SCALE

Bollards

Hatch covers from
above engines

Cross bollard

ORIGINAL SKETCH BY JOHN LIDDIARD / ILLUSTRATED BY MEURIG REES

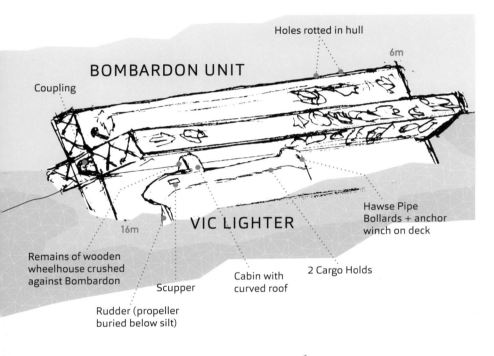

Holes rotted in hull

6m

BOMBARDON UNIT

Coupling

VIC LIGHTER

Hawse Pipe
Bollards + anchor
winch on deck

16m

Remains of wooden
wheelhouse crushed
against Bombardon

2 Cargo Holds

Scupper

Cabin with
curved roof

Rudder (propeller
buried below silt)

N

THE LANDING CRAFT
& BOMBARDON UNIT

50.34.419N 02.24.986W

OUTER BREAKWATER
PORTLAND HARBOUR

OUTER BREAKWATER
– PORTLAND HARBOUR

PHOTO: WILL APPLEYARD

Location
Portland Harbour, between the eastern and southern entrances

Getting There
Portland or Weymouth based dive centres. Using your own boat – head straight out across Portland harbour toward the southern or eastern entrance and pick a spot along the outer wall.

Depth
Wall top to 18 metres

Things to look out for
Very big spider crabs & bottles thrown from the old military buildings. The Beatles.

Dive blown out?
Visit Underwater Explorers' "ship wreck project"
underwaterexplorers.co.uk/ theshipwreckproject

Some may turn their noses up at this dive site, however we could not help but include the outer breakwater in this book… "Because it's there"! Portland harbour is one of the largest man made harbours in the world and the construction of it began in 1849. Local dive centres will drop divers along its outer wall as a local drift dive. Huge boulders make up the wall and slope to a depth of 18 metres. This boulder habitat is populated by wrasse and blennies galore with velvet swimming crab and lobster residing within its structure. From time to time extremely big spider crabs make this area their home too. The seabed is extremely muddy – put your hand down to steady yourself and you will sink to at least the wrist. Tip: Add interest to the dive by drifting by "the beatles" – D Day remains of metal pontoons that supported "road ways" between Mulberry harbours. A small section of these now sunken pontoons can be found just south of the middle / eastern harbour entrance, at the foot of the wall. Take a torch and you may discover a conger or two living within. Along the top of the harbour wall between both entrances on the east side sits a series of abandoned military buildings and sentry posts, from here military personnel have discarded bottles and crockery, some of which can still be found on the seabed today. Other breakwater dive possibilities include drifting back into the harbour from

the middle / eastern entrance behind the "chequered fort" and into the "secret harbour". John Dory can be seen here and on occasion, a lone seal has been spotted. At the southern entrance to the harbour rests the wreck of WW1 battle cruiser HMS Hood – avoid this area at all costs as the wreck is incredibly unstable. The Hood, as it is known locally, was deliberately put there to protect ships within the inner harbour from the threat of German U Boat torpedoes.

THE
⊙ 50°34.054'N 002°25.491'W
DREDGER

THE DREDGER

50°34.054´N 002°25.491´W

Location
Just outside of Portland Harbour's southern entrance

Getting There
Portland based dive centres are closest. A quick whizz across the harbour by RIB

Depth
10 metres (On a deep day)

Things to look out for
Plaice on the sandy seabed, lone Lump Sucker, the harbour wall and of course the wreck

Dive blown out?
Pack your climbing shoes and go bouldering on Portland.
rockfax.com

This dive is perfect for the novice diver

PHOTO: WILL APPLEYARD

Not a huge amount is known about The Dredger or how it came to be where it is in Balaclava Bay. It is a very easy dive accessible by boat, sitting in only ten metres of water just outside the harbour wall. It is well broken up consisting of metal plates and steel remains jutting out from the sandy bottom in every direction. Fish life is plentiful for such a shallow and simple wreck, with decent shoals of bib and pollack taking refuge in every nook and cranny. The site will not take you long to explore and it is made up of two main areas of wreckage. Head in a northerly direction towards the harbour wall in order to add interest to the dive and take a torch, as the boulders that make up the harbour wall are quite big, creating a cave like habitat for all manner of critters. This dive is perfect for the novice diver and due to the lack of current here and its shallow proximity means visibility is usually quite good.

BALACLAVA BAY
(BALLY BAY)

BALACLAVA BAY
(BALLY BAY)

Location
Just outside of Portland Harbour southern entrance

Getting There
Portland or Weymouth based dive centres run trips. Using your own boat – launch from Castletown, head toward the southern entrance of Portland harbour and the bay is to your right as you exit.

Depth
10 metres

Things to look out for
Scallops

Dive blown out?
Take a look at Portland Bill Lighthouse and the wild waters that pass it *trinityhouse.co.uk*

the real attraction for divers here is the opportunity to collect scallops

Bally Bay is a good training site or introduction to UK diving. The wreck of the Dredger sits by the harbour wall in the same bay, however the real attraction for divers here is the opportunity to collect scallops. The seabed is made up of a mixture of sand, rocks and weed. Snake lock anemones are everywhere and pipefish can be spotted here also. This dive site is often used as a second dive on a two-dive hard boat package or perhaps a local bimble from a RIB. Following the coastline southwest brings you to deeper territory where drift dive sites such as the "Cannon Ball Run" and Grove Point" are situated. Head east on your dive in Bally Bay to take you to deeper water, head west for a shallower dive.

PHOTO: ROB ROSLYN

SS
⊙ 50°32.122'N 02°20.088'W
BINNENDIJK

149

SS BINNENDIJK

50°32.122'N 02°20.088'W

Location
Shambles bank, east of Portland

Getting There
Portland or Weymouth based dive centres or launch from Castletown

Depth
26 metres

Things to look out for
Cargo of tyres & copper wire, the stern section

Dive blown out?
Go for a wild walk through Studland
isleofpurbeck.com/studland

The 1921 built SS Binnendijik or "Benny" as local divers and fisherman call her, was part of a trio of vessels sent to the seabed by mine laying German U boat U26. U26 also put paid to the near by Elena R and the now popular wreck of the Alex Van Opstal. The 6873-ton Dutch cargo ship came to grief in 1939 en route from New York to Rotterdam and therefore one of the first maritime casualties of WW2. Today she lays broken up in around 26 metres of water on the Shambles bank, east of Portland. The wreck has been well salvaged, however parts of her remains are still recognisable, especially the stern section. Other parts of the Binnendijk stand seven to eight metres proud of the seabed. Her cargo of tyres and copper wire can also be found among the wreckage of which lays on and within the sandy seabed. With the dive site's location in the relative lea of Portland, this wreck can be dived when many others cannot. Diving on slack water however is essential.

this wreck can be dived when many others cannot. Diving on slack water however is essential.

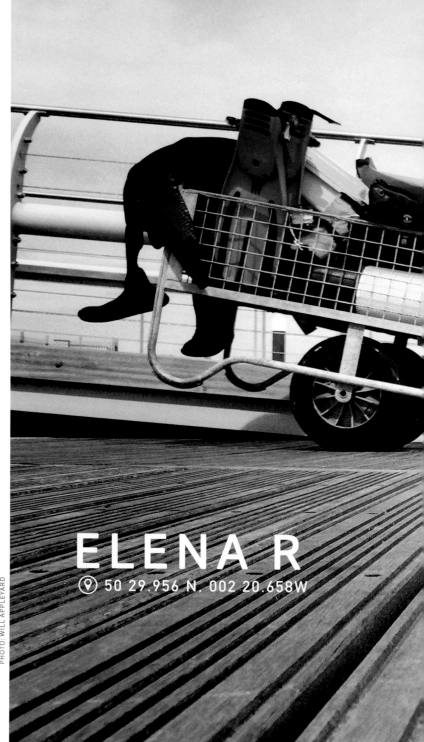

ELENA R

⦿ 50 29.956 N, 002 20.658W

ELENA R

50 29.956 N. 002 20.658W

Location
Shambles bank, Portland

Getting There
Boat charter or launching from Portland will be your quickest route. On the Shambles bank.

Depth
23 - 28 metres

Things to look out for
Amidships is where the action happens on this wreck.

Dive blown out?
Get muddy instead on a quad bike! *henleyhillbillies.co.uk*

Greek cargo ship the "Elena R" is said to be one of three vessels sent down by WWII mine laying U Boat U26 on 22nd November 1939. The other two victims being the Binnendijk and the Alex Van Opstal. Today the Elena R's remains entertain divers and fishermen alike sitting on the Shambles bank – a large strip of coarse shifting sand lying just off the tip and east of Portland. Fierce currents rage here, so it is essential that the site is dived on slack water. Tip: Often the visibility is good here, but often great on a neap tide. The vessel was 370 feet long and has been well salvaged, however there is still plenty of wreckage to explore – particularly amidships. Here the boilers are still visible in part and large square sections

PHOTO: WILL APPLEYARD

of the engine room hatches make up the most interesting areas. Elements of this area tower four metres or more above the seabed and if diving here on air with a single cylinder you will manage two or three laps before your bottom time sends you back to the surface. Other areas of interest include the remains of her mast, the bow section (where the anchor and chain are still visible) and the rudder. Stacks of lobster and crab live here and schools of every species of British fish are evident. Tompot Blennies appear to plague the place and conger eels will be found in their holes glaring out at passing divers. Watch yourself on snagged fishing gear and consider picking up any jettisoned beer cans that appear to be present on the wreck. In anything other than flat calm weather the boat ride to the site can be lumpy, especially in a RIB. This wreck however is worth the journey.

Fierce currents rage here, so it is essential that the site is dived on slack water.

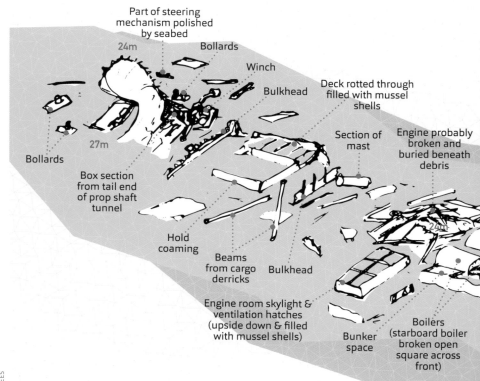

Part of steering mechanism polished by seabed

24m

Bollards

Winch

Bulkhead

Deck rotted through filled with mussel shells

Section of mast

Engine probably broken and buried beneath debris

Bollards

27m

Box section from tail end of prop shaft tunnel

Hold coaming

Beams from cargo derricks

Bulkhead

Engine room skylight & ventilation hatches (upside down & filled with mussel shells)

Bunker space

Boilers (starboard boiler broken open square across front)

N

ELENA R
50 29.956 N, 002 20.658W

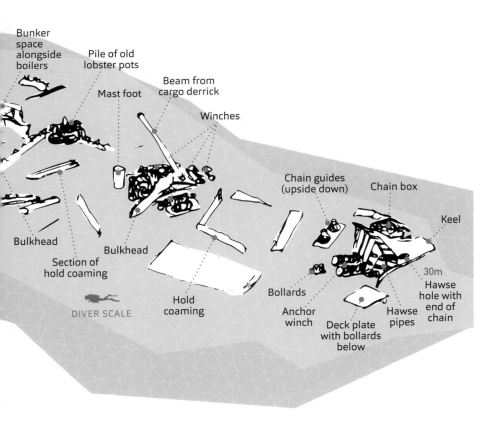

Bunker space alongside boilers

Pile of old lobster pots

Mast foot

Beam from cargo derrick

Winches

Chain guides (upside down)

Chain box

Keel

Bulkhead

Section of hold coaming

Bulkhead

DIVER SCALE

Hold coaming

Bollards

Anchor winch

Deck plate with bollards below

Hawse pipes

30m

Hawse hole with end of chain

PULPIT
⦿ 50°30.630'N 02°27.800'W
ROCK

PULPIT ROCK

50°30.630'N 02°27.800'W

Location
South west of Portland Bill lighthouse

Getting There
Either a shore dive, which is a quite an expedition, with a tricky entry and exit – head for Portland Bill lighthouse on Portland (Portland Bill Road), nearest sat nav DT5 2JT. Or by boat from Portland based dive centres. 25 minutes by boat.

Depth
7 – 30 metres

Things to look out for
Gullies, ledges and big boulders teaming with life. Topside - rock climbers along Portland's cliffs can be seen here and there en route to the dive site.

Dive blown out?
Peruse the dive shop at Scimitar Diving *scimitardiving.co.uk*

The skipper's knowledge of the site and its tides is essential.

PHOTO: ROB ROSLYN

If travelling by charter boat from a local dive centre or launching your boat from the east side of Portland your boat ride should take between 15 and 25 minutes depending on the sea state. Pulpit Rock itself is an unmistakeable natural landmark and affords a superb backdrop to the dive you are about to experience. The skipper's knowledge of the site and its tides is essential, as for most of the day a fierce current rips through this area. There are a couple of ways to dive this site, start shallow nearer the cliffs at around 8 metres eventually making your way deeper through the rocky labyrinth to around 30 metres, or have your skipper drop you deep from the off where you are more likely to chance upon plaice in the sandier part of the seabed. As well as the abundance of crab and lobsters, scorpion fish can be seen here too, lolling about on weed covered rocks and gullies. Keep one

eye out for lobster pot lines (a snagging hazard) as this is a popular area among the fishing community. The gargantuan amount of water that passes Pulpit Rock during the non dive-able part of the day (which is most of it) means that the area is nutrient rich, attracting more marine life than many other sites in the area. It is possible to dive by Pulpit Rock straight from the shore too, however this could be considered more of an expedition owing to the effort required to get to the entry point with your gear and indeed out again. One should stay close to the rocks if diving this site from the shore, so as not to get swept away by strong currents. The area is popular with spear fisherman too, so keep an eye out for groups of stealthy looking guys in camouflaged wet suits attached to their orange buoys breaking the surface from time to time. This part of the coastline is also interesting to explore from the shore, so if time is on your side, park up by Portland Bill lighthouse and go and have a scramble about on the rocks.

AERIALS
(DRIFT)

PHOTO: WILL APPLEYARD

AERIALS
50.32.761N 002 27.388W

PHOTO: WILL APPLEYARD

Location
Portland – west side

Getting There
Boat charter or launching from
Portland will be your quickest route.

Depth
8 – 20 metres

Things to look out for
A critter-hunt among the ledges
and boulders

Dive blown out?
Visit The Bournemouth Aquarium
Oceanarium.co.uk

Known locally as the "Aerials" owing to the MOD owned aerials that were once visible along the west cliffs of Portland above this scenic dive site. Now all that remains of this activity is a series of MOD buildings sat close to the cliff edge. Diving here is largely dependent on the tides, with often a raging current charging past this western side of Portland for much of the day. When the tide does slacken off, start your dive closer to the cliffs at around eight metres. Here you will drop onto predominantly kelp, but head west and eventually the seabed will begin to shelve off producing a more interesting environment of weed-clad rocks. Explore deeper still and the weed subsides to reveal impressive boulders, which create interesting passageways for the diver to fin through. At a depth of 16 - 18 metres the boulders become fewer and further apart, making way for larger patches of sand and the visibility in this area is regularly eight metres or more. Heading further west and deeper again may take you into the current as the area becomes more exposed. Surface marker buoys are essential when diving on this side of Portland.

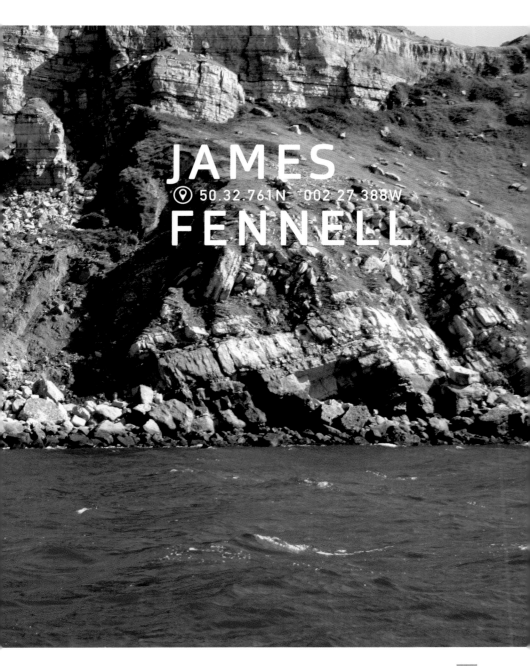

JAMES

50.32.761N   002.27.388W

FENNELL

JAMES FENNELL

50.32.761N 002 27.388W

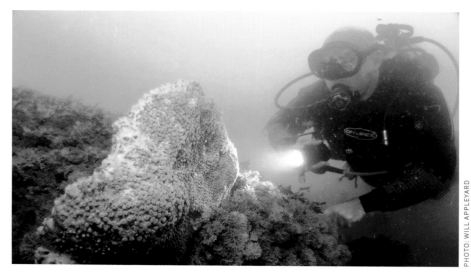

PHOTO: WILL APPLEYARD

Situated only a hundred or so yards from
the wreck of the Gertrude, the James
Fennell, formerly a trawler is now a wreck
site popular with Portland & Weymouth
based dive centres. The remains sit in a
concentrated area but stand three metres
proud of the seabed and are easy to identify.
The James Fennell ran on to rocks owing to
fog on 16th January 1920. All of the crew
escaped the stricken vessel. The boiler is
the most prominent part with the engine sat
directly behind creating a little swim through
between the two main parts. Head towards
what was the stern and two blades from
the propeller stand proud of the sea floor.
Outside of the wreck area consists of a big

Location
Clay Ope

Getting There
Head round the Bill from Portland
or Weymouth or steam across
Lyme Bay.

Depth
15 metres

Things to look out for
Boiler, engine and propeller in that
order. Keep an eye on the rocks for
nudi branch and pipefish.

Dive blown out?
Perhaps the eastern side of
Portland is not!

boulder field and a sandy seabed. Yellow "boring sponges" add a splash of colour to the rocks and small numbers of pink sea fans live here in places. Pipefish have been seen in the area as well as several species of nudi branch. The wreck is slightly exposed to currents so better to dive here on slack water. If the current picks up and is heading west, you may eventually find yourself on the Gertrude wreck. The area should be completely avoided with a strong westerly wind blowing.

GERTRUDE

50°32.819'N 02°27.242'W

GERTRUDE

50°32.819'N 02°27.242'W

Location
Portland

Getting There
Boat charter or launching from
Portland will be your quickest route.

Depth
6 – 14 metres

Things to look out for
The boiler and the remains
of the hull.

Dive blown out?
Fly over to Abbotsbury Swannery
Abbotsburyswannery.co.uk

PHOTO: ROB ROSLYN

This is a cracking little shallow dive site. Take in the views as you circumnavigate the whole of the Isle of Portland, past the famous lighthouse, then on to Pulpit Rock and eventually past Tar Rocks where the Gurtrude's wrecked remains now live. The dive will start shallow at around six metres and shelves down gently to around 14. Although this is a reasonably small site, many parts of the former vessel are still recognisable. The immense boiler appears to tower above you in the relative shallows and evidence of the propeller drive shaft still remains here also. The ship's ribs jut out from the boulders in parts and are still clad with plates that once made up the ship's hull. The wreck has been a feature here since she drove ashore on 26th August 1894 as a result of thick fog – the same story behind many of the wrecks in the area. Once you have finished with the metal parts of the dive, explore further afield where the seabed is made up of a mix of kelp, boulders and in the deeper areas – patches of sand. The site is often home to hunting John Dory and the usual British sea critters are prolific in summer months. The Gertrude is a great beginner's dive site and the boat ride to and from your adventure on a flat calm day is a real bonus. The area is not affected by the tides and is sheltered from all but westerly winds. Chesil Cove is only round the corner, but launching your own boat from here would be difficult.

CHESIL COVE

CHESIL COVE

Location
West side of Portland

Getting There
Head towards Portland along the A354 / Portland Beach Road. Straight ahead on all roundabouts, drive up Chiswell and unload gear at the top of Brandy Row where the ramp to the beach begins.

Depth
Shore - 18 metres

Things to look out for
Pipefish, John Dory hunting, ribbed wreckage from the Preveza.

Dive blown out?
Try this for size instead
goape.co.uk

For further reading and video on Chesil Cove diving visit: underwaterexplorers. co.uk/projectchesil

PHOTO: WILL APPLEYARD

The Cove can be dived in any state of tide, as currents are weak. The site is sheltered from most north and east winds but anything above a force 3 from the south or east creates a swell – making entry, but more importantly exit, somewhat difficult or impossible. The best areas to dive in the Cove with depths ranging from 6 to 18 metres maximum are between the disused sewer pipeline (which starts more or less in front of Quiddles cafe) and the area which falls across the famous Cove House Inn – where pebbles give way to sand patches and eventually the rocks of Portland. The best scenery, undoubtedly, is found in the 8-14 metre range among the rocks, pebbles and assorted wreckage which shelters an abundance of sealife – this happens to be right in front of the ramp entry point. Therefore the first dive we suggest is directly down from the ramp. Chesil Cove has numerous underwater "trails" but can easily be dived straight in-and-out like any other beach. Rule of thumb in the Cove is "out is west and home is east". If you ever get confused, just head east or 90 degrees and you will be sure to come ashore somewhere! Chesil Cove drops down steeply on entry and then in steps from 3 metres thereafter as it eventually bottoms out at around 12-14 metres, though depths can exceed 18m further out. From shallow to deep, the beach is made up of small to larger pebbles with rocks scattered here and there, then rocky reefs and rock outcrops which give way to patches of flat sand and eventually a sandy bottom further west and north west. Depending on season, the area up to the sandy bottom can be covered in seaweed and/or kelp whereas there is a more expansive kelp forest towards the south end of the beach. Parking wise, there are three small car parks to choose from as well as a few spots here and there along the roadside. Tip: Get there early on a sunny day to avoid the faff of finding a space – it gets busy. Air fills and kit hire can be obtained from a number of local centres (see directory). Wildlife wise, you will be sure to see John Dory here picking off juvenile fish, occasional triggerfish and plenty of crustaceans during the summer. The Cove House Inn is a great spot for a post dive bite to eat and pint of local ale, or if arriving in the morning, why not treat yourself to the best pre-dive breakfast in Dorset at The Blue Fish Café.

PHOTO: WILL APPLEYARD

PHOTO: WILL APPLEYARD

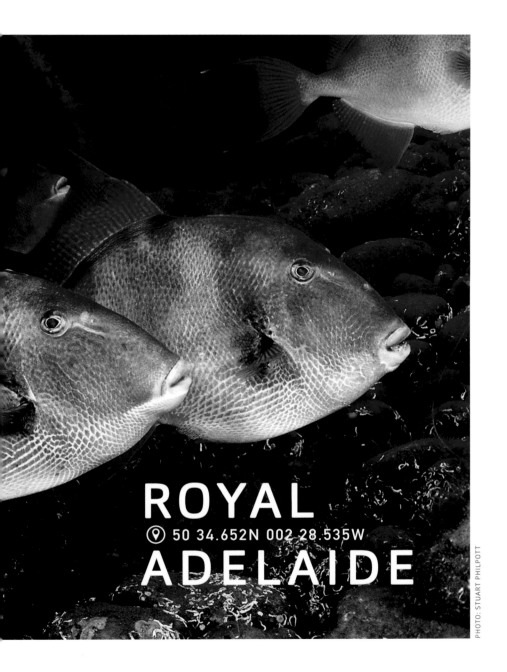

ROYAL
📍 50 34.652N 002 28.535W
ADELAIDE

ROYAL ADELAIDE

50 34.652N 002 28.535W

Location
Chesil Beach
(Chesil Beach Centre, A354)

Getting There
Hike over the beach from the Chesil Beach Centre car park. Align yourself with the first lamppost north of the car park entrance, head out to sea 150 Metres.

Depth
12 - 15 metres

Things to look out for
Grey trigger fish in summer

Dive blown out?
Check out some of these dummies at Nothe Fort *nothefort.co.uk*

This most underrated dive site is of course accessible by boat; however why not attempt the dive from the shore and inject a sense of "expedition" to your day. This 235ft iron sailing ship became wrecked on Chesil beach on 25th November 1872. Most of the crew were rescued, save for five and it is said that many onlookers assisted in "rescuing" the vessels cargo of gin too. It is also said that local folk proceeded to drink their ill-gotten gains well into the evening and by the morning the beach was littered with their dead bodies as a result of passing out drunk in the bitter cold of that night.

Dive wise - pack your lightest gear (forget twin sets) and park your car in the car park by the Chesil Beach Centre right by the main road, just past the Fleet. Cross the wooden footbridge and hike up and over the seemingly endless pebble beach. Entry will be difficult with a south-westerly wind blowing, but remember that exiting the water could be impossible in choppy conditions. Choose a flat calm day and set up a base on the beach and if possible with shore cover. The remains of the wreck lay approximately 150 metres off Chesil beach, roughly in line with the Chesil Beach Centre. The main area of wreckage covers an area of around 30 metres square and recognisable by the huge foredeck winch, anchor and chain. Parts of the starboard bow are visible with certain areas standing 4 metres proud of the seabed. There is no buoy to mark the wreck so a certain amount of hit and hope is required here. The site sits on a pebble shelf and effort to reach it is not only often rewarded with great visibility but during summer months, scores of grey trigger fish. It is thought that these guys travel up from the south Atlantic on the Gulf stream. These triggers are extremely inquisitive, so take your camera gear. As well as the trigger fish, pollack, gurnard, plaice, lobster and conger eel have all been spotted on the Adelaide.

UB74
📍 50°31.816'N 02°33.433'W

UB74

50°31.816'N 02°33.433'W

Location
West side of Portland

Getting There
40 minutes plus boat ride from Portland, Lyme Regis or Weymouth based dive centres. Also visited by West Bay based dive centres.

Depth
35 metres

Things to look out for
A large hole where the conning tower once stood. Huge conger eels peering out of wreckage. Your bottom time if diving on air. Climbers on the cliffs by Portland Bill.

Dive blown out?
Embrace that wind and learn to sail *moonfleet.net*

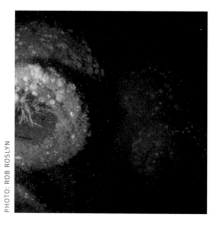

PHOTO: ROB ROSLYN

The wreckage of the UB 74 has been sat on the seabed just a couple of miles off the tip of Portland since 26th May 1918. This German U boat wreaked havoc with the allied fleet before being located and destroyed by depth charges. Since WW1 the U boat appears to have been heavily salvaged with the conning tower and propeller clearly missing. Where the conning tower once stood, divers are able to peer inside to find a tangle of her innards, however it is not open enough inside to penetrate. UB 74 sits on a sandy seabed at 36 metres and when in tact measured nearly 60 metres in length. The top of the wreck sits at around 31 metres. At one end the wreckage opens out to reveal more of the remains of her inner workings – here you may encounter one or two rather gnarled but content looking conger eels. Although perhaps not as impressive as the M2 submarine in her stature, this wreck still makes for an exciting dive site offering the recreational diver some reasonably challenging depth along with the chance to dive on a clearly recognisable (in parts) submarine. As well as the impressive conger eels living inside, the wreck is home to some pretty tame and sizeable cod and some fairly chunky looking crustaceans too. Diving on air you can fit in just one lap of the wreck before your bottom time runs out, however for maximum enjoyment take a bottle of nitrox with you. A RIB boat ride from Portland based dive centers or slipways should take roughly half an hour.

HMS M2

50°34.612'N 02°33.984'W

HMS M2

50°34.612'N 02°33.984'W

PHOTO: STUART PHILPOTT

Location
Lyme Bay

Getting There
Portland, West Bay or Lyme Regis based dive centres run shuttles.

Depth
20 - 33 metres

Things to look out for
One massive practically intact submarine, conger eels galore, big pollack and cod

Dive blown out?
Try karting instead!
southerncountiesleisure.com/karting

If travelling from Portland, the position of the dive site allows you to enjoy much of Portland's coastline on the way.

An intact 296ft submarine sitting upright in 35 metres of water, HMS M2 or "the M2" as it is known amongst divers, is an exciting wreck to dive. She tragically sank in January 1932 with the loss of all of her 60 her crew. The "M class" vessel was equipped with a small "Parnall Peto" sea going biplane with folding wings and it is thought that a fault with the plane's hanger door or perhaps the door being left open, led to her demise. The wreck is found a couple of miles off shore on the west side of Chesil

Beach in Lyme Bay, so it means with local dive boats launching from the east side of Portland harbour, the journey to the wreck can take 50 minutes. Dive centres from Lyme Regis and West Bay also run boats to the dive site. If travelling from Portland, the position of the dive site allows you to enjoy much of Portland's coastline on the way. Once in the water and descending the shot line, the impressive sub will appear from the gloom at 20 metres if landing right on the conning tower or 28 metres if you land on the pressure hull (deck level). If you make your way to the seabed, you will find yourself at 32-33 metres. Navigation of the wreck is easy, with your only options being stern to bow and back (or vice versa depending on where the shot has put you). You can follow the shot line all the way to the seabed (take a good torch) and explore the underside of the wreck, or stay at pressure hull level increasing your bottom time. The impressive conning tower and hanger are clearly identifiable with the hanger (always teaming with fish) being the only penetrable part. Avoid entering any other part of the M2, as not only is it full of silt inside but still contains the remains of her crew and so is a protected wreck. HMS M2 is a haven for all manner of marine life from conger eels, cod, crustaceans and starfish, to brightly coloured sponges and dead men's fingers. Jewel anemone decorate each side of the conning tower and you will see more tompot blennies on this wreck than on any other. The visibility can vary from a challenging two or three metres in the dark, to a glorious ten plus with the wreck laid out for you in all her glory. The M2 is a spectacular dive site so worth taking a camera and many UK divers will want it featuring in their logbook many times over.

PHOTO: RAF MUSEUM

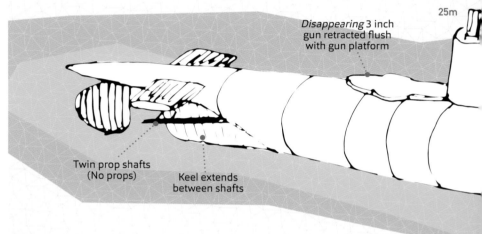

20m

25m

Disappearing 3 inch
gun retracted flush
with gun platform

Twin prop shafts
(No props)

Keel extends
between shafts

ORIGINAL SKETCH BY JOHN LIDDIARD / ILLUSTRATED BY MEURIG REES

HMS M2

50°34.612′N 02°33.984′W

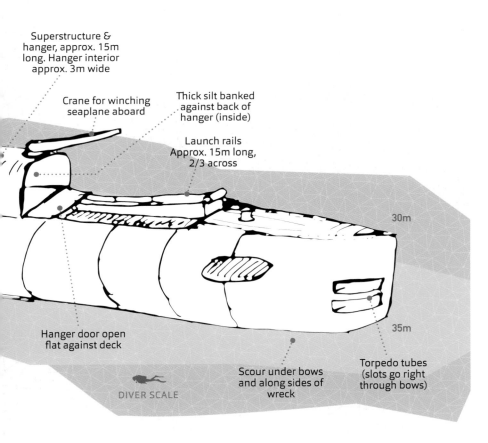

Superstructure & hanger, approx. 15m long. Hanger interior approx. 3m wide

Crane for winching seaplane aboard

Thick silt banked against back of hanger (inside)

Launch rails Approx. 15m long, 2/3 across

30m

35m

Hanger door open flat against deck

DIVER SCALE

Scour under bows and along sides of wreck

Torpedo tubes (slots go right through bows)

OVERALL LENGTH 90M

FROGNOR

📍 50°32.028'N 02°33.131W

FROGNOR

50°32.028'N 02°33.131W

Location
Lyme Bay, west of Portland

Getting There
Portland, West Bay or Lyme Regis based dive centres

Depth
35 metres

Things to look out for
A multitude of massive lobster

Dive blown out?
Bournemouth Karting
Matchamskarting.co.uk

PHOTO: WILL APPLEYARD

The Frogner, a Norwegian steamer (and also a borough of the city of Oslo) was stopped in her tracks by a torpedo fired from German submarine UC-17 on 29th April 1918. She sits at a depth of 35 metres in Lyme Bay, west of Portland. This wreckage, it seems, is home to the biggest and largest population of common lobster anywhere along the Dorset coastline. When diving on wrecks and reefs elsewhere in Dorset lobster often scurry back in to their holes or under the nearest piece of wreckage when curious divers approach – not here, these guys are massive and certainly not afraid of divers. The wreck provides an abundance of over hangs to poke about in and most certainly should be dived using nitrox if you can. It is a good one hour boat ride from Portland, so why not maximise your bottom time. The vessel was 260 feet long when sea worthy so lies over a vast area on the seabed.

This wreckage, it seems, is home to the biggest and largest population of common lobster anywhere along the Dorset coastline.

GIBEL
◉ 50°35'.851N 002° 53'.037'W
HAMAM

GIBEL HAMAM

50°35′.851N 002° 53′.037′W

Location
Lyme Bay

Getting There
Launch from Lyme Regis or West Bay. Hard boats typically take 45 minutes to reach her.

Depth
24 - 35 metres

Things to look out for
Bow and stern sections are prominent.

Dive blown out?
Blown out or not – go here!
theanchorinnseatown.co.uk

There does not seem to be any solid evidence proving exactly which German submarine sent the Gibel Hamam to the seabed on 14th September 1918. Records suggest that it was either the work of UB103 or UB104. Neither of those U Boats made it back home, so it appears that this German WW1 victory will remain a mystery. The only survivor (of the 22 crew) did report that a single torpedo quickly destroyed the coal carrying British steam ship by striking her on the port side amidships. The extent of the damage is evident today with her bow and stern being the most obvious parts of this wreck dive. The ship was en route

to France from Swansea carrying coal. A relatively small wreck at around 60 metres and formerly 647 tons, the boiler is still there as you would imagine and the highest parts of wreckage begin at 24 metres, with the seabed at 34 metres. Plenty of fish life here means that the wreck is popular with anglers too. This is evident as the site is festooned with lost fishing weights, lures and line. Care should be taken to avoid this tangling hazard and the wreck site given the respect that one normally would to a designated war grave. The diver pictured here is diving on the wreck exactly 96 years to the day she was lost.

SAW TOOTH
LEDGES

📍 50° 40.86'N, 002 48.15'W

SAW TOOTH LEDGES

50° 40.86′N, 002 48.15′W

PHOTO: WILL APPLEYARD

Location
Lyme Bay

Getting There
Boats or launch from West Bay or Lyme Regis.

Depth
25 metres

Things to look out for
A carpet of pink sea fans and soft corals. Gully & scallops.

Dive blown out?
Explore Lyme Regis
lymeregis.org

Imagine a sea floor before the age of destructive commercial scallop trawling, a seabed full of sea fans and soft corals... well imagine no further as (at the time of writing) Saw Tooth Ledges delivers just that. Designated a protective area stretching six miles out to sea from the West Bay area and several miles wide, free from scallop trawling Saw Tooth Ledges is named so due to the jagged appearance of the seabed. In addition, in places deep gullies have formed providing a haven for delicate fans and corals and more scallops per square metre than anywhere else in Lyme Bay. Upon reaching the seabed after free descending 25 metres the seabed will appear and the

PHOTO: DAMIAN BROWN

depth remains relatively constant save for the gullies and the slight rise and fall of the tooth like shelving sea floor. There are two types of dive here, a scallop dive or a scenic dive and local knowledge of the area will be required to put you on the desired spot. The scenic dive will see you exploring a more reef like habitat, while the scallop dive site provides a flatter seafloor to explore. Either way, the habitat provides divers with a reminder of what many areas of Dorset's undersea world should really look like. Let us hope that at the time of reading, Saw Tooth Ledges continues to remain a haven for this delicate and for most people - out of sight marine eco sytem.

PHOTO: DAMIAN BROWN

THE
📍 50°40'.532'N 002°56'.131W

HEROINE

THE HEROINE

50°40'.532'N 002°56'.131W

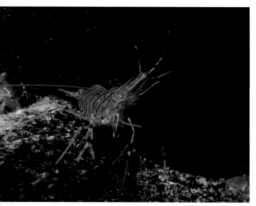

Location
Almost straight out to sea
from Lyme Regis

Getting There
Boat charter or launching from
West Bay or Lyme Regis

Depth
23 metres

Things to look out for
Bricks, bricks and more bricks.
LOTS of conger eels & prawns.

Dive blown out?
Dig out your hiking gear
and climb a "mountain"
(well, Golden Cap)
walkingbritain.co.uk

If you are looking for metal to dive on here, turn the page. If you are looking for a dive with the biggest family of conger eels for miles around – read on!

Originally a wooden sailing barque, the Heroine was bound for Australia in 1852 packed with emigrants hoping for a gold rush enriched life down under. However, come 27th December 1852 she found herself badly holed on rocks and fighting a losing battle in angry seas. It is said that the crew repeatedly fired the vessel's guns in order to successfully attract the attention of the inhabitants of Lyme Regis. A crew of five men bravely set off in an open boat towards the troubled Heroine and sadly four of those men died trying. Thankfully the crew and passengers did manage to escape the doomed barque and reach shore without loss of life. Today all that is left to see here wreck wise is a pile of "fire bricks" sitting under a layer of silt. Competent buoyancy is paramount here, as what may have started off as good visibility will quickly disappear with the mildest of fin kicks. Tip: Be the first diver off the boat and down the shot line for the best visibility. Along one edge of the pile a ledge has formed creating the perfect home for a dozen or more conger eels. Often sat in front of the eel inhabitants reside a concentrated colony of prawns. This area of the dive site is the main event and provides an excellent opportunity for keen photographers.

LANES
⊙ 50° 40.46'N, 002° 54.94'W
GROUND
REEF

LANES GROUND REEF

50° 40.46'N, 002° 54.94'W

PHOTO: WILL APPLEYARD

Location
Lyme Bay

Getting There
Three miles out from
Lyme Regis

Depth
24 - 29 metres

Things to look out for
Pink sea fans, sunset cup coral,
rose coral, hydroids

Dive blown out?
Learn more about the UK's
marine environment
www.marinephoto.co.uk

*Lanes Ground Reef is
an area rich in sponges
and marine invertebrate
filter feeders*

In July 2008 an area of 60 square miles of
Lyme Bay was declared closed to scallop
dredging and bottom trawling fisherman
and Lanes Ground Reef falls within this
exclusion zone. The ban, imposed by
DEFRA (Department for Environment Food
and Rural Affairs) was brought about to aid
the recovery of an important and fragile
eco-system. Lead by Natural England it was
demonstrated to the government that the
area was in desperate need of protection
and after many years of surveys conducted
in the area by various wildlife trusts and
societies the area was given the protection

it required. Lanes Ground Reef is an area rich in sponges and marine invertebrate filter feeders (ascidians). Many rare and unidentified species populate the reef and it is clear to see how this fragile environment can be quickly wiped off the seabed using destructive fishing methods. The reef itself consists of medium sized boulders and cobblestones and at a relatively constant depth of 24 metres. Sunset corals, rose corals, hydroids and pink sea fans now flourish here as well as the multitude fish species you would expect to find.

PHOTO: WILL APPLEYARD

PHOTO: WILL APPLEYARD

TENANTS REEF

⊙ 50 39.12 N 02 52.75 W

EAST

TENANTS REEF – EAST

50 39.12 N 02 52.75 W

PHOTO: DAMIAN BROWN

Location
Three miles south of Seatown

Getting There
Launch or charter boat from Lyme Regis or West Bay

Depth
18 - 29 metres

Things to look out for
A forest of fans, sponges & corals, boulders and rocky shelves.

Dive blown out?
Have a blast at Purbeck Shooting School
Purbeckshootingschool.com

Considered as one of the best scenic Dorset dive sites, two miles east of Tenants Reef West, Tenants Reef East is a dive site for those switched on by marine flora and fauna and macro lovers alike. As with Tenants Reef West, the pink sea fan is the star of the show and thrives in this habitat as do a variety of cold-water sponges, corals and anemone. These in turn provide the perfect habitat for hardly little critters and crustaceans. Fish life is in abundance on and above the reef, taking refuge about the boulders that make up the western end of the reef. Heading east, the reef begins to flatten out and shelve off before becoming a sandy seabed providing the perfect environment for scallops. The area in general is of scientific importance with "Reef Research" carrying out a study of this complex eco-system, of which we still know very little about. Reef systems of this quality are a rare find along the Dorset coast and we can only hope that they remain for many future generations of underwater explorers to discover and in turn protect.

Tenants Reef East is a dive site for those switched on by marine flora and fauna and macro lovers alike.

PHOTO: WILL APPLEYARD

TENANTS REEF

⊙ 50 38.82 N 02 57.70 W

WEST

TENANTS REEF – WEST

50 38.82 N 02 57.70 W

Location
4 miles south west of Lyme Regis

Getting There
Launch or boat charter from
Lyme Regis of West Bay

Depth
25 – 29 metres

Things to look out for
4 metre deep gullies, walls and
abundance of pink sea fans.

Dive blown out?
Abbotsbury Children's farm
should keep everyone happy
*http://abbotsbury-tourism.co.uk/
childrens_farm*

*West Tenants Reef
demonstrates the
diversity of diving
along the Dorset coast*

PHOTO: WILL APPLEYARD

Tenants Reef has been divided in to two areas
– east and west. Here, west Tenants being the
bigger of the two systems boasts up to four
metre deep gullies and rock walls decorated
with pink sea fans and soft corals. A haven
for marine life both areas often produce
bouts of excellent visibility. West Tenants Reef
demonstrates the diversity of diving along the
Dorset coast with this area being more akin to
diving in perhaps Cornwall in comparison to
anything else in its 95 miles of coastline. The

reef starts at around 24 metres and drops to 29 metres in parts so a free decent will be required once on the reef. The reef, stretching 1.5 miles east and west is thought to be the highest area of reef along the Dorset coast and said to be the origins of a prehistoric coastline, lost from site as sea levels rose millions of years ago. Expect a gentle drift dive here in usually weak currents and enjoy the seemingly endless display of sea fans as you float by the dramatic bedrock and seafloor.

WEST BAY

50° 42.40'N, 002° 48.91'W

HIGH GROUND

WEST BAY
HIGH GROUND

50° 42.40′N. 002° 48.91′W

Location
The ledge runs east to west, ¾ mile off shore.

Getting There
Dive charter from Lyme Regis or West Bay. Launch from Lyme Regis.

Depth
8 metres to wall top, drops off to 14 metres.

Things to look out for
A lengthy but shallow wall. Critters hiding within the wall.

Dive blown out?
Petrol head fun – Haynes International Motor Museum
Haynesmotormuseum.co.uk

The dive site runs east to west parallel to the shore and is quickly accessible by boat from either Lyme Regis or West Bay.

PHOTO: WILL APPLEYARD

Often seen as a decent second dive following something a bit deeper, this dive site should be described as more of a "ledge" than a "wall" dive. Once the plankton bloom has disappeared and after a spell of good weather, the visiting diver may often be greeted with superb visibility here. The ledge begins at around eight metres and drops off suddenly to somewhere in the region of 14 metres. Take a torch and spend an hour gliding along the ledge, seeking out the resident critters within the over hangs as you go. The dive site runs east to west parallel to the shore and is quickly accessible by boat from either Lyme Regis or West Bay. Admire the stunning Dorset scenery as you surface while waiting for your boat ride back to dry land.

ST DUNSTAN

⊙ 50°38.296´N 02°42.050´W

ST DUNSTAN

50°38.296'N 02°42.050'W

Location
Lyme Bay

Getting There
Launch from Lyme Regis or West Bay. Hard boats will visit from Weymouth and Portland too (closer to West Bay).

Depth
25 - 30 metres

Things to look out for
Dredging buckets, upturned bow, propeller, the engine-room.

Dive blown out?
Abbotsbury Sub Tropical Gardens
abbotsbury-tourism.co.uk

PHOTO: WILL APPLEYARD

A small wreck, the St Dunstan will accommodate a single boatload of divers nicely

In many cases shipwrecks of the Dorset coastline take a familiar form, with the boiler being the main area of interest and often the most recognisable of the ship's remains. In the case of the St Dunstan, the wreck offers the diver a little more than that. Sunk in 1917 by mine laying U Boat UC21, the St Dunstan lays in Lyme Bay with the bow section upturned. It is thought that she turned turtle when struck by the mine and now creates an entry point between two huge boilers and into the engine room. Here many of the inner workings and controls are still in place. It is a bit of a squeeze and should only be attempted if you are up to the job. It is also possible the follow the propeller shaft in from the other side of the up turned bow. Amid ships, much of the hull has fallen away, however the remaining propeller

shaft will lead you towards the stern where the propellers and rudder are in situ. A small wreck, the St Dunstan will accommodate a single boatload of divers nicely and with sections of her standing 5 metres proud of the seabed, the wreck accommodates decent sized shoals of bib and Pollack.

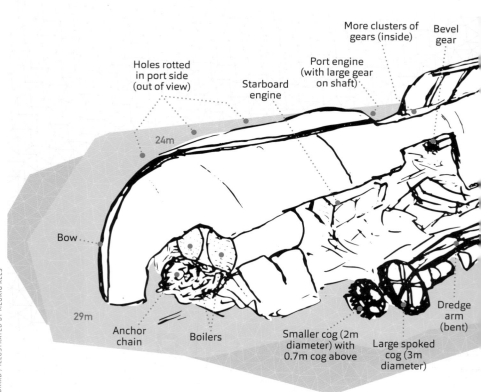

More clusters of
gears (inside)

Bevel
gear

Holes rotted
in port side
(out of view)

Port engine
(with large gear
on shaft)

Starboard
engine

24m

Bow

29m

Anchor
chain

Boilers

Smaller cog (2m
diameter) with
0.7m cog above

Large spoked
cog (3m
diameter)

Dredge
arm
(bent)

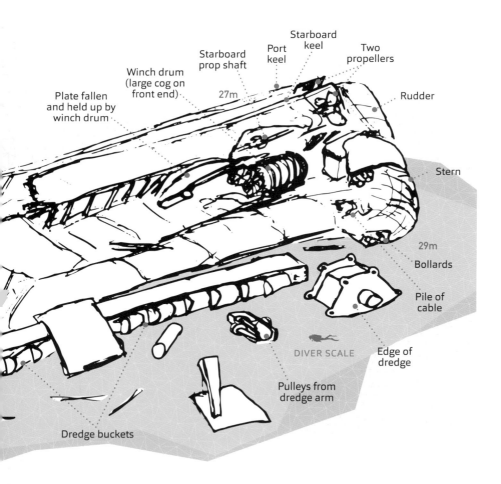

Plate fallen
and held up by
winch drum

Winch drum
(large cog on
front end)

27m

Starboard
prop shaft

Port
keel

Starboard
keel

Two
propellers

Rudder

Stern

29m

Bollards

Pile of
cable

Edge of
dredge

DIVER SCALE

Pulleys from
dredge arm

Dredge buckets

ST DUNSTAN

50°38.296'N 02°42.050'W

SS MOIDART

⊙ 50°34.043'N 02°47.282'W

SS MOIDART

50°34.043'N 02°47.282'W

📍 **Location**
7 miles from Lyme Regis

☞ **Getting There**
Boats from Lyme Regis, West
Bay, Portland & Weymouth all
visit the wreck.

🖐 **Depth**
28 - 33 metres

👓 **Things to look out for**
Both the bow and stern
sections

✋ **Dive blown out?**
Check out where all this began!
thedinosaurmuseum.com

WW1 and WW2 German torpedoes have provided divers along the Dorset coast with many wrecks to explore and SS Moidart is no exception. On 9th June 1918 German submarine UC77 despatched the coal carrying steam ship en route from Barry, Scotland to Rouen, France with the loss of 15 lives. The wreck lays in 33 metres of water with the shallowest parts (bow and stern deck) between 28 and 30 metres. It is worth studying the wreck map in this section closely before you dive her, particularly if you wish to explore both parts - for navigational reasons. The bow section still carries the anchor while the now separate stern section once carried the gun with only its mount remaining. The gun was recovered and sent off to the National Maritime Museum for restoration. Many of the decking ribs are still in place as well as several cargo winches and of course the boiler and several bollards. In good visibility the visiting diver can really appreciate the layout of this wreck with plenty of cover for marine life to make its home. The Moidart, pebble dashed with dead men's fingers sits in very close proximity to the wreck of its neighbour the "Ailsa Craig".

PHOTO: WILL APPLEYARD

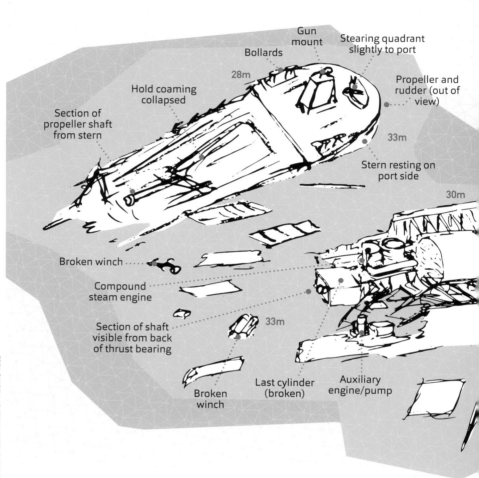

Gun mount

Bollards

Stearing quadrant slightly to port

28m

Hold coaming collapsed

Propeller and rudder (out of view)

Section of propeller shaft from stern

33m

Stern resting on port side

30m

Broken winch

Compound steam engine

Section of shaft visible from back of thrust bearing

33m

Broken winch

Last cylinder (broken)

Auxiliary engine/pump

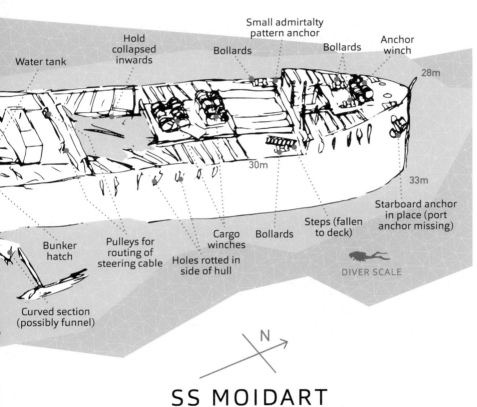

Water tank

Hold collapsed inwards

Small admirtalty pattern anchor

Bollards

Bollards

Anchor winch

28m

30m

33m

Starboard anchor in place (port anchor missing)

Steps (fallen to deck)

Bollards

Cargo winches

Holes rotted in side of hull

Pulleys for routing of steering cable

Bunker hatch

Curved section (possibly funnel)

DIVER SCALE

N

SS MOIDART

50°34.043'N 02°47.282'W

BAYGITANO

50°41.787'N 02°56.051'W

PHOTO: WILL APPLEYARD

BAYGITANO

50°41.787'N 02°56.051'W

PHOTO: WILL APPLEYARD

Location
1.5 miles from The Cobb, Lyme Regis

Getting There
Launch from Lyme Regis harbour (busy in summer) or jump on a charter boat with West Bay Diving or Blue Turtle.

Depth
20 metres

Things to look out for
Large boilers plus a smaller donkey boiler. Triple expansion steam engine and enormous shoals of bib.

Dive blown out?
Stay dry instead and check out – *lymeregismarineaquarium.co.uk*

The Baygitano has all the ingredients for a great UK wreck dive. Deep enough to make you think about your bottom time diving on air and enough recognisable remains left to play on - some of which stand six metres proud of the sand / gravel seabed. The 3073 ton armed collier was sent below the waves from a torpedo fired by UC-77 on 18th March 1918. Of the crew, 35 men were able to abandon ship while two were not so lucky. Today, divers will often begin their tour at the two main boilers amidships which are accompanied by a smaller "donkey boiler". Aft of the boilers you will find the ship's engine and beyond this a break in the wreckage. Fear not as just a few fin kicks later, if staying aligned with the propeller shaft, you will find a pair of water tanks, winches and the vessel's spare propeller sitting on what is left of the stern section. Evidence of the railings are also visible at the stern along with part of a mast. One or two areas of the wreck are penetrable including a section at the bow, however care should of course be taken in questionable visibility. Marine life wise it is said that the bib population outnumbers any other on the Dorset coast. Some sizeable spider crabs frequent the wreck and the resident congar eel is usually at home, so don't forget to say hello when when passing the boilers.

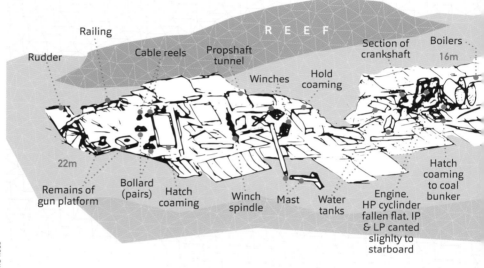

Railing

Rudder

Cable reels

Propshaft tunnel

R E E F

Section of crankshaft

Boilers

16m

Winches

Hold coaming

22m

Remains of gun platform

Bollard (pairs)

Hatch coaming

Winch spindle

Mast

Water tanks

Engine. HP cyclinder fallen flat. IP & LP canted slighlty to starboard

Hatch coaming to coal bunker

N

BAYGITANO

50°41.787'N 02°56.051'W

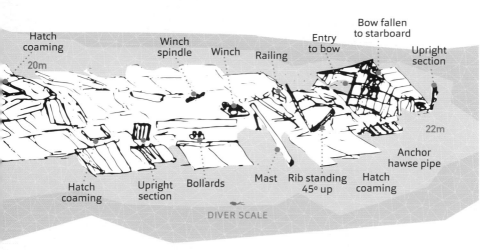

Hatch coaming
20m

Winch spindle

Winch

Railing

Entry to bow

Bow fallen to starboard

Upright section

22m

Anchor hawse pipe

Hatch coaming

Upright section

Bollards

Mast

Rib standing 45° up

Hatch coaming

DIVER SCALE

GOLDEN CAP
BOULDER FIELD

PHOTO: WILL APPLEYARD

GOLDEN CAP BOULDER FIELD

PHOTO: WILL APPLEYARD

Location
In front of the towering cliffs of Golden Cap

Getting There
This would be an ideal shore dive, however launch your boat or charter from Lyme Regis or West Bay. It is a trek along the beach!

Depth
7 - 15 metres

Things to look out for
Boulders! Crab and lobster. Golden Cap.

Dive blown out?
Blown out or not – go here!
theanchorinnseatown.co.uk

the site affords plenty of natural light for photographers and a pleasant bimble against the dramatic Golden Cap.

An ideal second dive to a two-tank day, the "boulder field" often attracts those wishing to take something home for tea. Among the boulders in shallow water live a thriving community of edible crab and a wealth of lobsters. Ideal for the beginner or divers wishing just to pootle about the rocks, the boulder field is a popular dive with minimal or no current present. In just a few metres of water, the site affords plenty of natural light for photographers and a pleasant bimble against the dramatic Golden Cap. An imposing lump of golden cretaceous sandstone, Golden Cap is the highest point on the south coast. It is worth carrying out the dive simply to be in its company and on a clear day, from the top it is said you can see Dartmoor. This would be an idea shore dive, save for the arduous trudge along deep shingle beach – definitely take a boat!

*To produce this book, we dived
with the following companies...*

DIVERS DOWN

SWANAGE BOAT CHARTERS

SCIMITAR DIVING

SABRE BOAT CHARTERS

Sabre Boat Charters

WEST BAY CHARTERS

West Bay Diving

Super special thanks!

Red Flannel Publishing, my inspirational Dad, DUKD divers Rob "WBT" Roslyn, Al Turner, Graham Wimble, Sara Clarke, Tim Berry, Damian Brown & Helen Phillips. Smudge for your enormous generosity, Dave & Oona @ Scimitar, Sarah Payne, Keith & Slim @ West Bay, Charters, Pete Tallack @ Sabre Charters, Pat & Pete @ Divers Down, Bryan & Martin Jones @ Swanage Boat Charters (brill maps Bryan). Simon Faithfull, Cordelia Chapman, Clare Butler, Roger Hoyle, Chris Ringrose (for modeling). Izzy Imzet (Chesil Cove copy), Paul Rose, John Liddiard & Stuart Philpott for your fantastic contributions. Sean, Marcus, Josh, Dave & Tom @ O'Three (thanks for the clobber). Portland Marina Harbour Master, Pipsy McGuire, Scott & Jace, Meurig Rees for your design wizardry & John Gilsenan for your initial design concepts. Charlie Grimwade, Blue Fish Café (the best breakfast in the county), The Harbour Lights, Dorset Gold and other ales. Khazana Contemporary Indian Cuisine! Rest in peace Mum.

ABOUT THE AUTHOR

Will Appleyard is a diver who has a passion for the waters of the UK and he communicates this enthusiasm through his photography and his writing. His first book "Discover UK Diving" has become a best seller and has raised the awareness of many dive sites off the south coast of England. Further afield Will's diving trips regularly take him to Europe, the Red Sea, Canada and to Thailand, but he is always pleased to return to home waters.

Will is not only an accomplished diver, but can often be found scaling heights as well as descending the depths. His recent climbing activities have taken him from the cliffs of Portland to the summit of Mont Blanc.